Marc "Animal" MacYoung

FISTS, WITS, AND A WICKED RIGHT

Surviving on the Wild Side of the Street

PALADIN PRESS
BOULDER, COLORADO

Also by Marc "Animal" MacYoung:
Cheap Shots, Ambushes, and other Lessons:
  A Down and Dirty Book on Streetfighting and Survival
Floor Fighting: Stompings, Maimings, and other Things to Avoid
  When a Fight Goes to the Floor
Knives, Knife Fighting, and Related Hassles:
  How to Survive a *Real* Knife Fight
Pool Cues, Beer Bottles, & Baseball Bats:
  Animal's Guide to Improvised Weapons
  for Self-Defense and Survival
Street E&E: Evading Escaping, and Other Ways to Save Your Ass
  When Things Get Ugly
Violence, Blunders, and Fractured Jaws:
  Advanced Awareness Techniques and Street Etiquette

Fists, Wits, and a Wicked Right:
Surviving on the Wild Side of the Street
by Marc "Animal" MacYoung

Copyright © 1991 by Marc "Animal" MacYoung

ISBN 0-87364-611-8
Printed in the United States of America

Published by Paladin Press, a division of
Paladin Enterprises, Inc., P.O. Box 1307,
Boulder, Colorado 80306, USA.
(303) 443-7250

Direct inquiries and/or orders to the above address.

PALADIN, PALADIN PRESS, and the "horse head" design
are trademarks belonging to Paladin Enterprises and
registered in United States Patent and Trademark Office.

Illustrations by Marc "Animal" MacYoung

CONTENTS

INTRODUCTION		1
CHAPTER ONE	*Blows*	13
CHAPTER TWO	*Shedding*	45
CHAPTER THREE	*The Noggin*	53
CHAPTER FOUR	*The Throat and Neck*	77
CHAPTER FIVE	*The Body*	93
CHAPTER SIX	*The Limbs*	121
AFTERWORD		145

If you don't get the fuck out of my face, I'm going to hit you until you're thin.

—William "Buzz" Lange

I t was one of those one-punch affairs that I seemed to have always found myself in when I was younger. All of our friends were there, and one of us had looked at the other cross-eyed. Well, when you're young and tough, that's all it takes some-times, so it had started up. After the preliminary woof-ing and posturing, stud muffins had decided it was time to swing. But because he had broadcast his moves so badly, as his blow landed, so did mine.

I've got to admit the boy's punch was harder than mine, but that's not the reason I stepped back. He looked at me with triumph in his eyes for about five seconds, thinking I was backing down. Thing was, I had stopped to get set for another round. A couple of things signaled to him that something was wrong: one, I wasn't really backing down; and two, his eyes were beginning to tear. Through all of the adrenaline and attitude, the message that he was in some serious pain was beginning to creep in. In fact, the pain sensors were downright annoyed with the load they were carrying right then. He began to waiver, and his friends stepped in with the usual, "Hey man, it's not worth it" and such. Thus ended one of my fights.

Okay, so the guy had pegged me a good one in the face. Straight shot to the left side, impact on cheek and upper jaw, missing the nose. His blow was harder than mine. He was young and tough and in pretty good shape. With all this, why'd he quit?

It could have had something to do with the fact that my blow had been a hook to the back of the jaw, right where it connects to the skull. Aside from the fact that the blow jerked his jaw sideways (a way that it doesn't usually move too well), it had slammed pressure into a cluster of nerves where the jaw meets the neck, just under the earlobe. His nervous system was going bonkers in pain, while I only hurt a little bit. My blow had *hurt* more.

Most people not only don't understand the physics of a good hit, they don't know *where* to hit either. That's the other half of knowing how to hit. I admit that there are people who can smash a person's face with one blow, but I ain't one of them, and I'm betting that you ain't either. That means you're going to have to do what I do and replace quantity with quality when it comes to blows. Okay, so you can't break boards with a single punch. Boards don't move or hit back—opponents do. This is something you're going to have to deal with if you intend to keep from getting your ass kicked too often in this lifetime. This calls for a little practice, accuracy, planning, and knowledge. Three of these you're going to have to work on and perfect yourself. The fourth, knowledge, I can give you. So you get a freebie.

Unlike most authors on this subject, I'm not going to give you a long-winded, pompous dissertation on theory. I know from personal experience how much it fuckin' hurts to get nailed with well-targeted blows. I'm going to try and streamline not only where the targets are, but the reason these blows hurt and their short- and long-term effectiveness. I'm also not going to lie to you about the effectiveness of these moves. In every book I've ever written on self-defense, I've stressed one major point: *"There ain't no guarantees in a fight!"* It depends on who you're up against, how well trained he is, his physiological makeup, what his mental state is, how tight you are with your blows, and a whole shit-load of other things.

There are certain things you can't control in a fight (like a Samoan for instance), and the only way to deal with these things is not to fight at all. There are terrible stories about people who can get kicked in the balls and they just get mad. They're true. I have both kicked someone and been kicked in the balls with that effect. Later on the pain and nausea show up, but at the time it's just infuriating. Part of the reason most formally trained martial artists lose in a fight is that somewhere in their little noggins is the belief that if they do A, B, and C, the other guy's going to go down. As we all know, bikers can be a little shaky on their ABCs, so instead of going down they pick up a bar stool and proceed to do a tonsillectomy on King Karate.

Actually, most of what is taught in martial arts schools is only half the lesson. There's a reason for this. In the 1970s, the martial arts went off like a time bomb in America. They'd been around for years, ticking away quietly and doing their own thing. All of a sudden, with the help of a pack of mercenary movie producers, they exploded into the American consciousness. Under the leadership of a skinny little guy with two first names, the glamour and glitz of Hollywood became the fantasy of a generation. What was it going to be? The quiet, skinny runt who kicked the shit out of the armies of evil lords? Maybe the quiet, peace-loving renegade holy man who, in spite of long dialects about peace and harmony, managed to stomp about five guys a week. How about the ex-special-something-or-other Vietnam vet turned cop? This is the guy who always got partners and girlfriends greased so he could go on a one-man rampage and wipe out evil drug czars.

With this kind of incentive, people went out and started getting martial arts training. Somewhere along the line they began to notice something: the bad guys weren't cooperating. They weren't dropping like flies to flurries of feet and fists. In fact, they were exhibiting tendencies at the opposite extreme. Instead of hanging around and duking it out toe-to-toe, they'd just bust a chair across the would-be karate hero's teeth. The situation was, in a word, ugly.

In the rush to create instant Bruce Lees, a whole lot of stuff was omitted. In my opinion, much of the critical information that got 86'd was directly related to long-term survival—the kind of stuff you'd better know if you're going to use the martial arts in the long run. It's the equivalent of teaching someone how to shoot an M16 without including how to clear a jam. On a shooting range, you can get away with it.

In a firefight, however, where people are shooting back, you might as well lay down and die if you can't clear a jam, 'cause you're dead.

Movie fantasy ran aground on the rocks of reality when the the big mistake was made in American martial arts. Instead of accepting the fact that they had a whole lot more work to do (including re-examining what they had dropped and really learning the tenets they professed to follow), they opted for the most face-saving way out and turned the martial arts into a sport.

Tournaments rapidly become the way of American martial arts. Since not everybody is interested in participating in the kumite (what the movie *Bloodsport* was about), they began to drop even more from the agenda. The information on where to hit to cause internal damage began to be filtered out. In time, "martial arts" became nothing more than a glorified contact sport. The problem with that is that eventually the jocks took over. These guys don't know what is missing from what they've been taught. What's worse, they never acquired "street etiquette," so they're still cocky. Sure, they can throw a devastatingly fast punch—they can throw six or seven of them. B.F.D. (big fuckin' deal). If their punches don't land in key spots, one well-placed sucker punch from a knowledgeable streetfighter is going to do more damage. The way to win a fight is not to be able to hit faster (or even harder), but to cause more damage to the other guy first.

The flip side of this is that if you know what hurts, you can protect those key spots with a little more gusto. It's my personal belief that when you're first learning self-defense it's more important to keep from getting hurt than it is to be able to hurt somebody else. Contrary to what those franchised karate schoolteachers and the movies like to promote, the guy is going to fight back. If he does, there's a really good chance you'll get hurt. To add insult to injury, not only is he going to fight back, you don't know how he's going to do it.

Now, I've spent a considerable amount of time in my life having the snot rattle around in my head from getting punched. It comes from having a big mouth and traveling a lot. The big mouth is obviously why I landed in fights in the first place. The traveling part is only obvious if you've done it. There are parts that just don't take kindly to outsiders, where folks think that your being a stranger means they can fuck with you without any repercussions. Cops are more prone to side with the locals (even if they're in the wrong) in the event of a fight.

The other thing that has led me into a number of altercations is a certain way I have of carrying myself. Before I earned the "Warrior's Mark," a lot of fights happened for no better reason than the fact that I had opened the "door of violence" in my reality. Since I've gone through some nasty shit, people are less likely to cross me for trivial reasons. It's no longer a game for me, and this is something people can sense. The door is still there, but there's a sign over it stating that going through it is going to cost you a piece of your ass. (Not *might* cost you, *will* cost you.) This is what I mean by the Warrior's Mark.

When I was younger, I fought a lot. Then I went through combat and the world changed for me. Now I make a big distinction between fighting and combat. And unless you're into having extended visits in places with names that end with "Men's Correctional Institution," you should not only learn, but *live*, the difference. I got in a whole slew of fights when I was younger, but that's all they were—two guys swinging away at each other until one backed down. Combat is where you can't back down. You are fighting for your life, and you go until one of you is either dead or hurt so badly that he can't go on.

I can't begin to explain what combat does to you. There's a major change in how you look at the world. What's more, it affects how people deal with you, and not always for the better. (In fact, for the most part it's in a negative way.) There's something in the way a person who's been in combat moves that comes through. In fact, I've spent most of my life learning how to deal with it. It's no small problem, so I'd advise you to not to be too hot about earning this Warrior's Mark.

The truth is, for all our society applauds John Wayne, it has no system for acceptance of warriors. Look at all the guys who are still fighting what Vietnam did to them. The society that sent them had no way to incorporate them back into the normal flow. That's probably why more vets have committed suicide since getting back than were killed overseas. Sobering thought about becoming a so-called warrior, isn't it?

What this leads up to is the point that there really are better things to do with your time than fighting (like getting laid, for instance). Unfortunately, the sorry state of affairs is that we can't spend all of our time getting our dicks wet; sometimes this means we waste time fighting.

It is also true that there are people who are more interested in slugging people than making love. Every now and then you will have the bad luck to encounter one of these warped individuals. These people are masters of sucker punches, painful shots, and low blows. The shit you'll learn about in this book is the stuff they love to pull. That's why I'll also talk about how to counter it and how to avoid it.

The information in this book should change your opinion of fighting from a macho game to a serious

responsibility. The knowledge that you can permanent-
ly hurt or kill someone should always ride with you
when you're heading toward a fight. A fight doesn't
end when your opponent hits the floor. Cops, revenge,
a change in social standing (not always for the better),
family vendettas, courts, and prison can and *will* play
a part in the aftermath. If you go out and misuse this
information you'll be setting yourself up for more trouble than you can imagine. It really is a matter of playing the odds. Sooner or later there's going to be a bullet
in the barrel. The less you misuse this information, the
better the odds that the bullet won't have your name
on it.

This knowledge is part of hanging the shingle over
the door I mentioned earlier. Violence is like a door
into your space. Most people don't even know the door
exists. What it comes down to is sheer dumb luck when
the animals outside don't find that door into your reality. I used to hate people who would laugh at me
about violence. They thought they were untouchable.
Let me say something right now, across the board:
*Nobody is untouchable. Anybody can be touched by vio-
lence!* Those fuckers who were laughing were sitting
there with nothing but air between them and violence.
Social behavior and rules mean nothing when you're
outside the particular group that empowers you. If
somebody decides to rip your throat out, there is nothing between you and him but your skills and talents.
Once violence has been decided upon, all of the rules
that normally govern people's actions become smoke
in the wind. This is what I mean by the door of violence. Until you know about this door, you can't lock
it. Until it's locked, there's nothing keeping the animals
outside where they belong.

What you'll learn in this book is the equivalent of
opening the door and looking outside. When this hap-

pens, some people scream and try to run away, but in their haste they leave the fucking door open and the animals outside start coming in. These are the people who, by knowing about violence, invite it in. Another kind of person opens the door and then builds a bunker inside with M60s and grenade launchers pointing out the opening. The problem with this system is that you are stuck on guard duty from then on. Other people go out the door and learn about the terrors of the territory outside. Of these, most never make it back. I was one of the lucky ones.

It's the people who know how it works out there that can do something about that damned door. The first thing they do is paint a shingle with the Warrior's Mark and hang it up over the door. This tells the animals outside that there is something inside that leaves claw marks higher up the tree than they do. This wards off about 90 percent of would-be troublemakers. The next thing somebody in the know does is go inside, slam the door, and lock it! Then they proceed to get on with their lives. Anytime somebody comes knocking on that door, they answer it with a shotgun in hand and an attitude to match. Anyone trying to break in will get blown away right off the bat.

That's what the sign tells the dirtbags if you have it posted: you're not going to mess around. You're not on their turf, and they ain't invited onto yours. That's what I write about—painting that sign, locking that door, and getting on with your life.

Now another thing I stress is that I don't know everything there is to know about fighting. Nobody does. And unlike other so-called experts, I'm not here to sound like I piss lightning and shit marble. I don't give a rat's ass about proper form or how many tournament trophies are on the shelf. I'm talking about real streetfighting here. This is something I've come to know by getting knocked upside the head and having bullets whiz by me while diving for cover. Truth is, very few martial arts instructors have been in more than three fights. I've had that and then some.

Thing is, my dick ain't going to get put out of joint if you don't agree with what I'm saying here. No law says you have to take this book as gospel. It's your ass you're trying to save, and you've got to do what works for you. All I'm doing is giving you the benefit of my actual experience. I'm not telling you what to do, but I am giving you things to think about that might save your ass.

I'm not trying to promote my own personal style as the "ultimate martial art," 'cause it ain't. What's more, there ain't no such critter. What I am trying to promote is an understanding that there are two things you should know. The first one I've told you already— *"there ain't no guarantees in a fight!"* The second one is that *it's your awareness, wits, and fists that will keep you safe out there, not some fancy fighting form.* In time, your awareness is what is really going to save you, but in the meantime you may have to resort to fists. As you go along, you'll find ways other than fighting to deal with the shit, but for now you'd better know this.

Now I'm not into writing the same book over and over again. In fact, my other books all go together to form a whole course on self-defense. I recommend reading my first book, *Cheap Shots, Ambushes, and Other Lessons: A Down and Dirty Book on Streetfighting and Survival,* as a companion to this one. This book will stand on its own, but it's more of a technical manual on blows and targeting, while *Cheap Shots* is an overview of what you need to know to be truly good at self-defense. I'm going into details in this book that I didn't go into in *Cheap Shots.* Then again, this book doesn't have the scope that *Cheap Shots* did. For those of you who want to know about weapons and such, I cover those in my other books: *Knives, Knife Fighting and Related Hassles: How to Survive a Real Knife Fight* and *Pool Cues, Beer Bottles, and Baseball Bats: Animal's Guide to Improvised Weapons for Self-Defense and Survival.* If you're interested, read 'em. If not, fine—weapons are a serious drag any way you look at them. The info that's relevant to this book is in *Cheap Shots.*

If you've read my other books already, you know I'm not exactly a sterling example of white, middle-class attitude. Also, my name and the word "somber" ain't often heard together in the same sentence. I screw around a lot. What I'm talking about here is some painful stuff, so I keep it light whenever I can. It makes it easier for me to write and for you to read. Another thing I do a lot is talk about things that may initially appear to have nothing to do with self-defense. The thing is, they do. Most black belts will go down against a streetfighter because while the black belt is thinking about dropping into some fancy pose, the streetfighter is grabbing for the chair he's going to bust across the black belt's teeth. *Self-defense is mostly awareness and commitment.* A lot of what may seem to be useless babbling about unrelated stuff is actually me trying to give you the critical information that nobody else talks about—things that will keep you alive and intact, not chop socky, out in the street. Hell, it's a lot more fun knowing this sort of stuff so you don't have to fight. So kick back—if you're into it, crack a beer—and enjoy this book.

CHAPTER ONE

Blows

Oh shit . . .

—Me, to myself, after hitting Oberon with a blow that would have dropped a bull and having him calmly look at me while he decided whether or not to get mad.

I n my first book I went into the different types of blows in detail. Basically, I break down most of the blows that exist into four loosely defined categories that strikes of any style fall into.

The Four Biggies

- Setups
- Rattlers
- Maimers
- Nighty Nite Bunny Rabbits

Not the normal names for these things, but then again, who can pronounce the formal names? "Hieechi ebooboo thingamajig" sounds fancy, but when you get past all the lyrical lingo it all boils down to a swift kick in the nuts. That's the same in any language.

Some styles will stay in one category more than others, and therein lies a major weakness. Most of what is taught in America as karate stays in the Nighty Nite Bunny Rabbit (N.N.B.R.) category, while in boxing, Setups and Rattlers are the bread and butter. This explains why, nine times out of ten, a boxer will rip the shit out of a karate boy. Karate, while more powerful, is slower than boxing. The boxer will flit in, do damage, and then get the hell out of there. If the karate guy can land one, it's probably going to be effective (unless the boxer sheds it, but we'll go into that in the next chapter). By accepting the fact that he's in a fight that will take awhile to finish, the boxer won't try to nail his opponent with one shot. (Although I've seen people taken out by one shot, usually the guy who got creamed was more of a loudmouth than a fighter—he was lipping off when he should have been ducking.)

So what are the different types of blows?

Setups

Setups are usually light, fast blows. They carry little or no clout because they are generally thrown with the arms only; very little body weight is involved. For the most part, they get in and sting. They can lead you into chasing will-o'-the-wisps or they can unnerve you. While you're trying to block these mothers, something with a little more personality is usually getting ready to visit you (thus the name).

If you know where to strike, however, Setups can do

a little more than just sting. A Setup to the back of the jaw can count as much as a Rattler to the cheek. This is because the Setup lands in a tender spot, while the Rattler hits nothing but bone. The targeting makes the lighter punch more effective.

One thing that never ceases to amaze me is the number of people who don't think about strategy and tactics during a fight. They think a fight consists of a blindbull charge that finishes the guy off immediately. That's combat, not a fight. There's a big difference between the two. To keep it from becoming combat, you have to use your head. Thinking about strategy and tactics during a fight is where Setups come into play.

Rattlers

Rattlers are a bitch to deal with because of their middle-of-the-road position (sorta like Democrats—individually, they cause a little bit of damage, but collectively they can really fuck you up . . . jeez, these things really *are* like Democrats). They have more body weight behind them, which means they land harder than Setups but they're lighter and faster than N.N.B.R.s. When one of these mothers lands, it can rattle you a good one (thus the name). Wherever they hit, they're going to hurt. If they hit a key spot, they can bump up to N.N.B.R. status. This is what I used on the guy I told you about at the beginning of this book. I took a semipowerful blow and put it in a tender spot instead of on the frame, as he had done.

Maimers

Unlike the other blows, Maimers are done with the hand only. The others can be either punches or kicks. These suckers call for fingers and thumbs. The call is an ugly one. They are designed to rip parts off people, and they do it real well. About 99 percent of all

Maimers are aimed at the tender spots I'm going to talk about in this book, so you'd better keep a sharp eye out. Otherwise, somebody's going to do to you what Lyndon B. Johnson said about Hubert H. Humphrey: have your pecker in his pocket.

Nighty Nite Bunny Rabbits

Here they are, the infamous knockout punches and kicks. N.N.B.R.s are blows that either put somebody out of commission or seriously hurt him to the point that he either can't go on or doesn't want to do anything but go off and cry. The reason they are so effective is that the person throwing them is using all of his body weight to back up the blow. You don't want to be around one of these mothers at any time. If the guy knows where to target, it's going to be hospital time for sure (possibly even the morgue). I have seen people blown off their feet by these things. One guy I saw had his feet knocked at least two feet straight up off the ground by a N.N.B.R. to his head. We were about fifty feet away and we heard his jaw break. Needless to say the guy was asleep before he hit the floor. That is the best (or worst) example of what these blows can do when they hit the right target.

I did some research and discovered that bare-handed murders usually run neck-and-neck with the number of murders committed with clubs, hammers, and such. This should serve as a fairly good reminder of why you should pay attention to the different types of blows.

As you've probably guessed by now, the effectiveness of a blow can be improved by proper targeting. Somebody who knows where to hit can cause more damage with three blows than somebody who doesn't can with ten. That's why when I was in training we used to have a motto: "If the guy is still standing after three moves, get back and see what you're doing wrong." This is how much a blow can be improved by proper targeting. There are a lot of people out there who can do just as much damage as I can, if not more. If I'm talking about taking somebody out in three moves, you can imagine what the guy with a nickname like "One-Punch" can do. Someone who knows *where* to hit as well as *how* to hit is a motherin' bad combo to come up against.

Hand Positions

Let's move on to a slightly specialized field—how to hold your hand. Throughout this book I'm going to refer to punches with fancy names like Leopard, Phoenix, Hanging, and so on. I'm also going to talk about Bear Swats, Eagle Claws, Knife Edges, and related horseshit. I'm going to cover these up front so you don't wonder what the hell I'm talking about when I say something like, "A Leopard Punch to the bladder can really fuck up somebody's day." Which it can. Depending on A) how full the guy's bladder is and B) how hard you hit, it can either rupture the bladder and lead to toxic shock syndrome or just compress it and hurt like hell.

There are literally hundreds of ways to hold your hands when you strike. Some of the positions I'm going to show you fall into the Maimer category, although most float over to the Rattler/N.N.B.R. groups. The thing about most of them is they take a little practice before you can do them right. There are two basic reasons for this, and the specific hand position being used will determine which is more prominent.

First, they use different muscles than a regular punch. It's not that the wrist muscles aren't used, it's just that the impact comes in from a different sector.

In order to do these without breaking fingers or jamming joints, you have to practice and build up the muscles. If you slam out with a Phoenix Punch against somebody's temple you'll probably fuck your finger up. So a little practice first will save you a shitload of pain later.

The second reason you should practice beforehand is simple: targeting. You're aiming for pressure points, joints, appendages, and muscle groups. This means limited target size, and to add insult to injury, the fuckin' things are probably going to be moving. (The odds are that the guy doesn't know exactly what to protect, but if he's in the process of trying to hurt you, he's not going to be sitting there like a wooden dummy.)

Hitting somebody in the chest with a regular-fisted Rattler is about as useless as a fart in a tornado. First of all, it's impacting a major muscle group. Also, there's all sorts of bone to absorb the impact and distribute it throughout the frame. Finally, you're using too big of a striking surface. (I'll explain striking surfaces in a bit.) On the other hand, the same strength of strike delivered as a Leopard Punch to the area where the chest turns into arm hurts like a bitch. That's because there's less muscle there and the only bone is support frame. Best of all, the nerves and arteries get smashed. Believe me, it hurts like a motherfucker.

If you still want to, go ahead and throw a punch against the guy's chest. His kicking your ass will tell you more effectively than I can that it's a waste of time. Your other option is to accept that you've got a group of small, moving targets to aim for, and that means practicing for accuracy.

The next booger about these hand positions is that they involve something I mentioned earlier—striking surface. All the physics and shit aside, what this means is that the bigger the surface you strike with, the more distributed the impact will be.

For example, if you were to slap a wall with your open hand, the energy of the motion would be transferred into the wall over an area the size of the entire surface of your hand. All in all, there wouldn't be too much damage to the wall because of the size of the impact area. If, however, you were to take an ice pick and strike the wall with the same amount of energy, you'd stab a hole in it. This is what I mean about striking surface—the size of the area the energy is being delivered through determines the effectiveness of the blow.

Now, before you get any ideas about running out and doing a knockout punch using some of these hand positions, let's take a quick reality break. The amount of energy being transferred is still the same when directed at smaller areas, but it is concentrated and therefore more damaging. This is a very exciting concept, but there are drawbacks. The worst one has to do with breaking strength. It doesn't sound like too big of a problem until you realize we're talking about your fingers.

If you practice your ass off for ten years you might be able to knock somebody out with one of these smaller-strike-area blows without turning all of the bones in your hand into kindling. Most N.N.B.R.s are done with a larger striking surface because the amount of energy required is greater. The greater the amount of energy required, the stronger (harder, larger) the vehicle delivering it must be in order to withstand the job. An ice pick can go through a wall because not only does it cover a smaller, more concentrated area, but steel is harder than the drywall. If, however, you increase the force of the blow, you can blast a hole in the wall with your punch. But to do that you must increase the size of your striking surface to compensate for the extra energy. If you were to try and do it with your finger, you'd end up with something that looked like a fat caterpillar hanging off your hand.

There are all sorts of exceptions to what I've just said. For example, a hollow-tipped bullet is quite effective because it squishes. Problem is, it can't be used again. We're not talking about throwaways here; it's your hands and fingers on the line. There are demo martial artists who can poke holes in this, that, and the other thing using just their pinkies. I ain't one them, and neither are you. While it is possible to overcome the breaking point of a striking surface with speed, you have to be motherin' fast. This involves a streamlined motion and all sorts of other physics related to speed, angle, tensile strength, mass, velocity, ad nauseam. For the Average Joe, it's easier to remember one thing: the harder the blow, the bigger and/or harder the striking surface should be. If you're going to hit somebody really hard, don't do it with a hand position that is only effective up to a Rattler, because it will be out of its league. (Don't think the guy's going to stop and let you go see the nurse because you hurt your little hand, either.)

Let's look at the plain old fist. Yep, that's it. The mighty fist. The karate crusher, the boxer's beauty, the broken hand if you do it wrong, that one. Step One (it sounds stupid, but I have seen more people with broken hands because of it): *When you hit someone or something with a fist, tighten the muscles in your hand and wrist.* Literally, make a fist. A fist is not just a curled-up hand, but one that is held tight and is therefore hard! I have seen people cock back and slam somebody with all their weight and might and forget to tighten their hands. Not only do they bust

the other guy's face, they bust their hands. No lie—
I've seen it happen several times.

When I was a total fucking badass, I used to practice my punches on trees. I'd stand there for about
twenty minutes a day whaling on a tree. I never busted
my hand because I always kept the muscles in my
hand and forearm rock-hard. So when I hit someone or
something, I did it with a very hard surface, which
served as an added incentive not to fuck with me. I
also used to practice by hitting walls and columns. In
time, I developed calluses on my knuckles that were so
thick I could put out cigarettes on them and not feel it.
(A great way to keep someone from fucking with you is
to take the cigarette out of his mouth and grind it out
on your knuckle while looking him dead in the eye.)
Once, I walked into a "martial arts room" at a gym I
had just joined, and all these cockstrong bucks were
sizing me up while doing all kinds of showy kicks.
There was something about me they weren't comfortable with, and they were working themselves into a
frenzy because they felt threatened. The more threatened they felt, the flashier and louder they got. I knew
it was only a matter of time before somebody worked
up the guts to cross me. I put an end to those ideas
when I walked up to a steel I-beam and started ham-
mering on it. Ten minutes later I had the room to
myself.

I could do that sort of thing without incurring damage because I had enough muscle tension in my hands
and arms to absorb the impact and pass it along. I also
had "grounding," which I have mentioned in other
books. So most of the impact was being passed through
me and into the ground. (For most of you this is down
the line a ways, but be aware that it is coming.)

There are several schools of thought on hitting
and which part of the hand to use. There are a whole

shitload of contentions as to which one is better, as with everything else in the martial arts. (This is what happens when something is turned into both a sport and an academic circle-jerk.) My personal belief is that they are all good in certain areas. Which one will be most effective depends on the situation you're in. That's the bottom line—selecting the right tool for the job. There is no one, all-encompassing, "right" punch.

There is, however, one pretty well agreed upon *wrong* way to punch, and that's with your pinky and ring finger. This is how most broken knuckles occur. They usually happen during hooks and swings, or with straight punches when the guy moves. Knuckles get broken most often when you strike with the thumb facing the ground. A lot of the bullshit that is taught as karate in this country promotes this kind of blow. If you're striking at a flat stationary object, it's fine and dandy. If you're striking at a cylindrical surface (like a face) that's moving, you're in a risky area.

The way around this is to target your punches as well as you would with a small-strike-area blow. Strike at the centerline. If, for instance, you're nose-to-nose and striking at somebody's face with a straight punch, aim for the center of the face, not the cheek. That way, if the guy moves aside, you're still going to hit him with full force, but on the cheek, not in the center of the face. If, however, you target his cheek with a straight punch and he moves, only part of your hand is going to hit—a glancing blow at an angle you're unprepared for. Remember what we discussed about reduced striking areas needing to be stronger? There you go. If you're going for the cheek, come in at an angle so the guy's cheek is the centerline of the approach vector. Look at the following illustrations and you'll see what I mean.

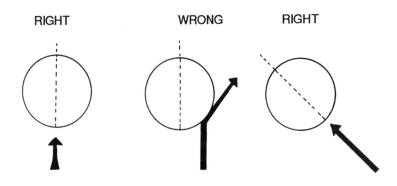

Blows coming in on and off centerline.

Okay, now we're ready to get into hand positions in depth. The different ways of punching consist of two different elements. One is striking surface, and the other is fist positioning. Let's look at striking surfaces first.

Striking Surfaces

One school of thought says the best way to punch is with the index- and middle-finger knuckles. In a sense, that condenses the striking surface into a smaller area. These punches hurt when they hit. Their drawback is that the wrist has to be held slightly bent to the outside to ensure that these two knuckles arrive first. The hairball is that if the guy sheds the punch (explained in the next chapter) you end up hitting with the ring and pinky knuckles. Oops.

Another school of thought says the entire front of the fist should be used as the striking surface. The wrist is held a smidgen off straight, and the impact is absorbed over a larger area. If you are throwing a N.N.B.R., this is the one to use. Your fist can withstand the impact better because of the larger area. The draw-

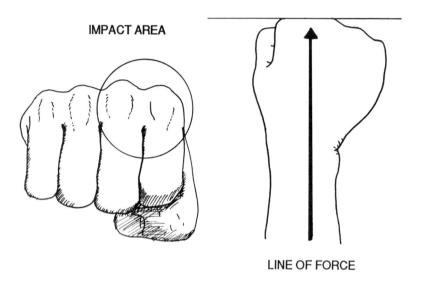

IMPACT AREA

LINE OF FORCE

Two-knuckle impact and wrist position.

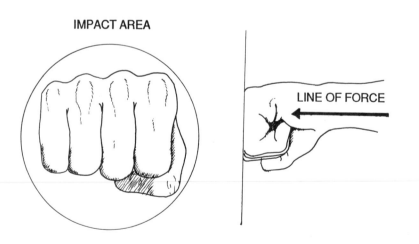

IMPACT AREA

LINE OF FORCE

Front impact and wrist position.

back is that on Rattlers and Setups, the impact to your opponent is diffused.

A third school uses the knuckles only. This is more of a barroom-brawl-type move. The wrist is held so that the knuckles land first. It hurts like a bitch when used with a Rattler or a Setup. Its weakness lies in the fact that the wrist is at a stress point upon impact and may fold up on you (read "possibly break"). I don't advise using it with straight punches. It's great for N.N.B.R.s, where the line of force is curved.

IMPACT AREA   LINE OF FORCE

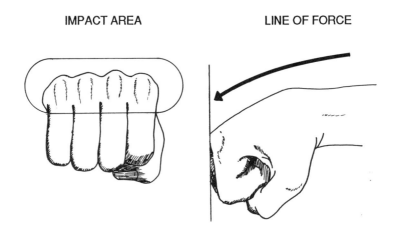

Knuckle impact and wrist position.

The other option you'll hear people going on about is what I call the Karate Punch. It's a thin, red cunt hair away from the "oops" position, so I have a hard time with it (as taught by most people). The Karate Punch uses the middle, ring, and pinky knuckles as striking surfaces. Believe it or not, this provides the closest thing to a clean and direct line of force for

IMPACT AREA

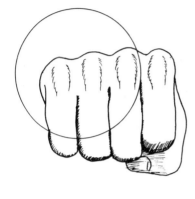

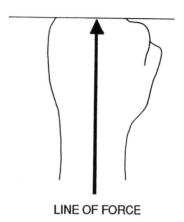

LINE OF FORCE

Karate punch.

IMPACT AREA

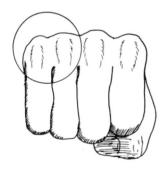

NO! WRONG!
ERROR 7!
BROKEN-HAND TIME!

LINE OF FORCE

Wrong way to punch.

your blow. Since the blow comes from the elbow, there is no bend in the wrist to act as an energy sink against it. It's a powerful punch, but I advise against using it with your hand in a horizontal position (I'll explain this soon). That statement is going to put some people's panties in a wad, but remember, in a real fight it's hard to do everything in proper form. In fact, nine times out of ten, form goes down the toilet. That leads to busted knuckles because something that looked good on the drawing board didn't work in the field. When you're in the field, you should pay attention to what works in the field. When you're at the drawing board you can only fuss with the way things might be.

Fist Positions

Now that we have the striking surfaces out of the way, let's move onto fist positions, another area of hot debate. Actually, there are three hot ones while one is standard. The standard fist position that not too many people argue about is with the tip of your thumb pointing in toward your body so the blow to your opponent's body is delivered from beneath. For the most part, uppercuts are delivered using this position, although an underhand jab could use any of the four positions. Take a look at the illustration and you'll see what I mean.

Of the other three fist positions, each has strong points and drawbacks. (Do you ever get the impression that there ain't no guarantees in a fight? You're right. All sorts of little details must be thought about and contended with.)

The first one is with the thumb facing the ground. In case you got the impression earlier that I don't like this position, that's not exactly the case. I'm not sexually excited over it, but it has a very solid use. This puppy is great for massive body shots. I mean, if you're going to cave in someone's ribs or cause internal hem-

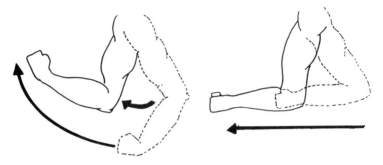

Uppercut and underhand jab.

orrhaging with a N.N.B.R., this is the gumby to use. If you're targeting the face and head, though, it's kind of easy to miss and hurt yourself if you're not careful. This position is the one the karate boys seem to like so much and, if delivered right, it *can* smash ribs. No shit. If you do it wrong, you can hurt yourself more than you hurt the other guy.

The second one is best with jabs, hooks, and anything coming in from the side. The hand is held at an angle off the arm. It's mostly for the knuckle-type striking surfaces, but not entirely. The angle can range from 35 to 55 degrees, depending on your preference. (There's probably a "correct" angle, but I don't know it.) This position is the middle-of-the-road way to hold your hand because it has the advantage of the vertical position (lessening the chance of a broken hand) and a good deal of the clout that the horizontal position carries. It's more comfortable for the person throwing it, which generally translates into increased speed. This is why this position is used often for Rattlers and Setups.

The third position is with the fist held vertically. This one is common in wing chun gung fu and some of the southern styles. The real bennie is that it makes it almost impossible to bust your hand with a glancing shot, namely because you aim for the centerline with this style of blow. (By the way, don't ever tangle with a wing chun-trained person in a narrow area. The system is designed for fighting in the cramped alleys of Hong Kong. The fuckers are wicked in confined spaces.) Bruce Lee's famous "one-inch punch" was derived from wing chun. (They had it for a long time; he just got all the credit for it because he supposedly invented it. Actually, all he did was introduce it to the West.) The drawback of this position is that it really feels funky until you get the hang of it, so it might slow you down some. Also it's mezzo-mezzo with anything but a straight punch.

HORIZONTAL   ANGLED   VERTICAL

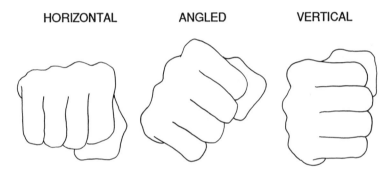

Three hand angles.

Muscle Tension

Another bone of contention among martial artists is muscle tension. Here's the rub: the looser the muscles, the faster the blow; the tighter the muscles, the harder the blow. Now mix in body weight utilization and you end up back at Setups, Rattlers, and Nighty Nite Bunny Rabbits. If you're totally relaxed and snake one out at somebody using nothing but arm, it's going to come in fast but light (Setup). If you tighten up and include some body weight, it's going to hurt, but it'll be slower (Rattler). If, on the other hand (wait a minute—I only got two hands) you lock it down and throw every ounce of your body weight into it, it's going to put the motherfucker to sleep (Nighty Nite Bunny Rabbit).

A mutant variation of all of this comes, once again, from wing chun. Everything is kept loose when the punch is thrown, but at the last second all of the muscles tighten down. That's what the "one-inch punch" is about. (I don't recall ever seeing it done to anyone in a Shao-lin forward horse; a horse stance is real weak from the side. Come to think of it, I've never heard of it being used against a boxer, either.) When the punch is thrown, it's coming in with the speed of a Setup. Yet, when it locks down, it suddenly becomes a Rattler, if not a N.N.B.R. Fortunately, this type of blow is kind of tricky to perfect so you're not likely to encounter it very often. On the other hand, it's a real grin to have up your sleeve.

I've just given you the basics of hand positions for punches. It's up to you to mess around with them until you find what's comfortable for you. You need to practice before you try to use these in a fight. The only way to learn it is to actually do it, because that's how you learn what it feels like when it's done right. That's something I can't tell you in a book. (By the way, if you ever have anybody—especially a Thai—hold out his arms with his fists facing you palmward, run. He's trained in Muay Thai, and he'll boot you into next week. Kickboxing is a retarded Western child of this form. These fuckers are serious. Until 1928 they were wrapping their arms in glue-coated rope and then rolling them in busted glass shards. These boys don't play light.)

On to specific types of punches. This is where all

the stuff I've bored you with thus far comes to fruition.

Punches

Here's where we get picky about striking surfaces, angle of impact, weight of blow, and so on.

Leopard

One of the blows you're going to hear me prattle on about a lot is a Leopard Punch. Oddly enough, it's from the Shao-lin animal styles. (I always thought it a hoot that a guy named Animal was learning the animal forms.) Unlike the Tiger, which will just rip the shit out of you, the Leopard will knock the shit out of you first, then tear you open to see if anything is left over. My old teacher told me about a slow-motion picture he had seen of a leopard catching a small boar. What first impressed him was that the leopard had hooked the boar with the claws on one paw to slow him down. (Okay so far—cat, claws, they sort of go together.) The next move was what was most impressive, though. The leopard cocked back and knocked the boar upside the head with his other paw. The impact of the blow stunned the boar long enough for the cat to finish it off in the usual cat manner—jaws and back feet.

By the way, in case you didn't know, when you're playing with kitty and he/she gloms onto your arm and then brings the back feet into play, what's happening is actually a disemboweling move. Cats rip the guts out of their prey that way. Along the same lines, those little, squeaky dog toys make the same sound a varmint makes when it gets killed by fang, claw, or impact. Our cute little pets have their eyes pointing forward, just like humans, and all other land carnivores, do. Interesting, no?

Anyway, enough biology. Back to punchouts. The Leopard Punch is delivered in a motion that's similar to a snake striking. The striking surface is the second knuckle set, a reduced striking area that makes the Leopard an extremely effective punch when thrown with the weight and speed of a Rattler. If targeted correctly it can act almost like an N.N.B.R., because it will hurt the guy so much that he really won't want to go on.

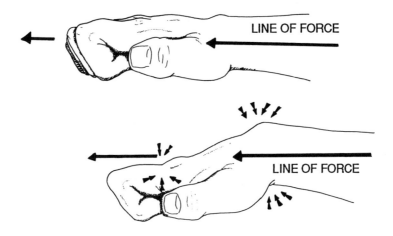

LINE OF FORCE

LINE OF FORCE

The correct way to throw a Leopard Punch (top) and the absolute, stone-cold wrong way (bottom).

With practice this can be a more accurate blow than a regular fist because of the reduced striking surface. The drawback is that in order to use it effectively you need to strengthen the muscles of the back of your hand, or your fingers will fold backward and your hand will roll up in a rather unpleasant manner. This is why, unless you have mucho training, you shouldn't try to throw this one as a N.N.B.R. That much energy will break your hand as well as his face.

Dragon

Another annoying strike is called the Dragon. It's a real bitch to take, because not only does it clobber you, it immediately puts the fingers in a position to start ripping. The impact is delivered with the palm of the hand, and the fingers are cocked back so that once the blow lands, the fingers dig in. Ouch. The difference between this and a slap is that a slap hurts less because it's delivered with the muscles of the hand relaxed. With this mother, on the other hand, the muscles are rock hard and ready to go. (Sort of sounds like another part of the anatomy, don't it?)

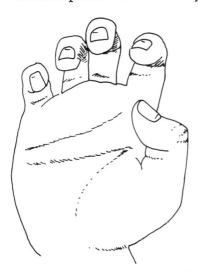

The Dragon is especially effective against tender spots. Not only does it hit, it rips. It can bring tears to your eyes right quick, provided it isn't in the process of ripping them out.

Usually, this blow will come to your address in a roundabout way, which is its one weakness, because a swing is easier to block than a straight punch or a jab (although it can and will come at you straight). When this happens it's a real pain in the ass to deal with. It can

Dragon Strike.

also come at you from underneath, in which case you know somebody is trying to steal your family jewels.

The best way to deal with these things is not to stick around to find out what the guy is trying to tear off. "Shedding" is a great technique to use if you want to prevent anything important from taking a walk. (See Chapter 2.)

Hanging Punch

Now one of the bar-none, nastiest things you can come across when it comes to punches is a Hanging Punch. (I've also heard it referred to as an Elephant Punch, and there are probably some other names for this one, too.) It's a plain old fist, but the wrist is held in a rather odd manner that makes the whole thing operate along the physics of an axe. (Some folks see an elephant's trunk here, so I guess that's why it has the other name. Could be, I dunno.)

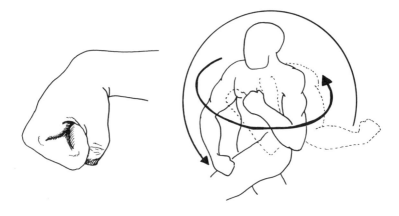

Hanging Punch (fist position and proper form).

With this type of blow, the question is which aspect is the worst to deal with. You have a wide choice of ugly. A true Hanging Punch comes in via an overhead arc, and these suckers use everything, including the kitchen sink, to increase the impact of the blow. Body weight, balance, speed, mobility, grounding, and muscle tension are all used to send you off to Lu-Lu land.

When I saw the guy have his feet knocked upward, this is the blow he got nailed by.

Another charming aspect of this is the hand position used, which makes it similar to an axe. Fighting an axe is a real bummer. Something about the physics of a right angle coming off a swinging stick increases impact capability. An axe can punch through armor that a sword bounces off. (It's true. I don't know why or wherefore, but it happens. If you can explain it, write me.)

Anyway, aside from these suckers landing harder, there's another serious bitch about fighting against an axe. It's one of those things that's easy to deal with once you know about it, but until then, you're going to get messed up by it. It has to do with reach. If somebody swings a baseball bat at you and you block it with another bat, that's fine and dandy. The point of impact, or where those bats strike, is also the point of threat. With an axe, though, if you hit the handle with a block, the point of threat is about six inches inside your guard. It's because of that angle. If you're fighting a straight object, its point of threat is limited to one line. An angled object can bring the threat inside your guard because your guard has more than one line to deal with. The point of danger is not where the blocking point is. (See the illustrations on the next page.)

Hanging Punches operate on the same principle. Here's an experiment you can try. With your wrists straight, put one arm in front of your face. Now arc your other arm up so that your arms hit one another in front of your face. Your arms should be crossed as the closer one blocks the blow. Look at the distance of the attacking fist from your face. Now, with the blocking wrist straight, bend the attacking wrist into a Hanging Punch and do the same. (By the way, make sure you block at least eight inches away or you're

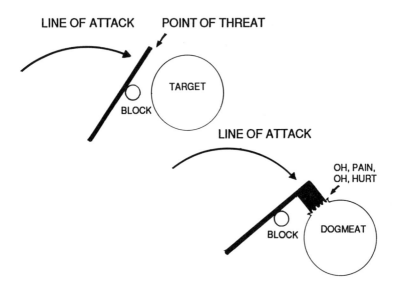

Stick striking point of block, and axe striking the same with increased point of threat.

going to pop yourself in the face.) Now you see why these mothers are a drag to deal with. With the increased reach, they can nail you before your block takes effect.

The way to deal with someone who is fighting with this kind of blow is to extend your guard about six inches. The same goes for kicks that use the balls of the feet, called "axe kicks." Contrary to what is taught in dojos, this is the more dangerous type of kick in the Setup and Rattler range. Kicks with the top of the foot are called "courtesy kicks" in that range. When it comes to N.N.B.R. kicks, though, the top of the foot is often used because the increased striking surface prevents a shattered foot.

I think I misled you with what I said a moment ago. It is true that you need to increase your guard six inches or so when the hand is held at an angle to the

arm. But when the hand is in this position it won't
always will be a Hanging Punch coming at you. This
hand position is also handy for hooks, jabs, and short
shots, and that's where you need to increase your
guard.

If the guy knows how to throw a Hanging Punch
correctly, there is only one thing to do: *get the fuck out
of the way!* A properly thrown Hanging Punch will
knock you into next week if you try to block it. (By
the way, in case there are any martial arts teachers
reading this and saying to themselves, "That's bullshit; I can block a Hanging Punch. I've done it in
practice bouts before," I have only one thing to say:
that's you. Can all of your students do it? Not just
your best—all of them. Come to think of it, the guy I
saw taken out was a two-time black belt. He was up
against a little guy from Thailand. Now what was
that answer again?)

A Hanging Punch is one of those mothers where the
guy cocks back into yesterday and starts a polar orbit
to bring you the bad news. So if you're in a fight and
you see something coming at you from overhead, *run
away.* The Chinese styles really like Hanging Punches,
so be careful.

Another type of blow that can knock you silly is
called a Bear Swat. A guy who taught self-defense in
Arizona showed it to me. He claimed it was from an
Indian fighting style. I think it was renamed into a
Japanese-sounding chulaka ryu. (I've yet to check up
on that one. I've seen it used since, but without any
name attached to it.)

It's basically a Dragon without the claws (or a
Leopard that's done with the palm instead of the
knuckles). The palm is the main striking surface, and
the fingers are curled back out of the way. It has many
of the same limitations as the Dragon, without the has-

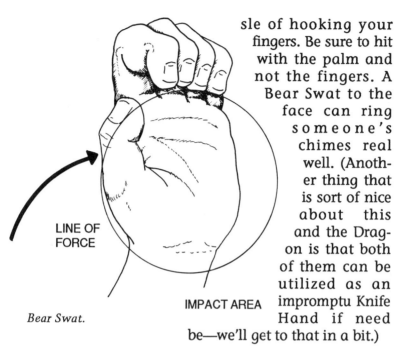

LINE OF
FORCE

IMPACT AREA

Bear Swat.

sle of hooking your fingers. Be sure to hit with the palm and not the fingers. A Bear Swat to the face can ring someone's chimes real well. (Another thing that is sort of nice about this and the Dragon is that both of them can be utilized as an impromptu Knife Hand if need be—we'll get to that in a bit.)

Palm Strike

Okay, the next one is a doohickey called a Palm Strike. Palm Strikes are like punches but they don't involve the fist. Their advantage is two-fold. First, believe it or not, the palm is the hardest part of your hand when it's cranked back like so.

The second thing that makes them rather neat is that you're not losing energy into the wrist joint. The impact is backed by the forearm itself. With a regular punch, if you have a weak wrist or haven't tightened it down when you punch, you can sprain or break it. This happens when your wrist folds up on you because you've put too much energy into the punch for the muscle tension to handle. Oops.

Palm Strikes are able to carry a whole shitload of clout, but there is one thing: you have to be sure to hit

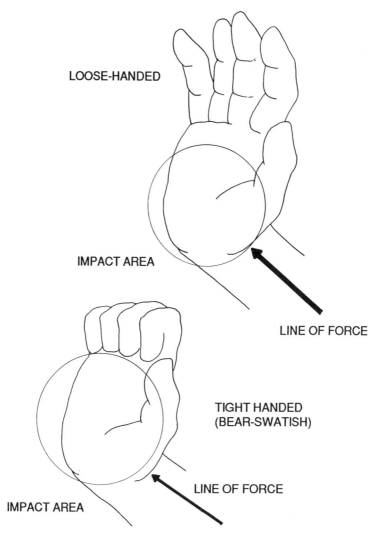

LOOSE-HANDED

IMPACT AREA

LINE OF FORCE

TIGHT HANDED
(BEAR-SWATISH)

LINE OF FORCE

IMPACT AREA

Palm Strike, loose-handed and Bear-Swatish.

with the part of the palm that's in front of your wrist (your lower palm). This is the part of the hand that can take the impact. If you strike with the fingers or the upper palm, your wrist will bend back and either break or sprain. Because of this, most Palm Strikes come from below or horizontally. (Striking at a downward angle isn't the hottest idea because you're going to hit with your fingers first. Breaky breaky, not good.)

There are two ways of doing these: loose-handed and tight-handed. Loose-handed looks like you're waving bye-bye at someone, while tight-handed looks like a Bear Swat that's tweaked at a weird angle. Don't try to mix these or you'll end up dislocating your fingers. Keep your hand either loose so the fingers can spring or tightly curled so the impact can be transferred elsewhere.

Done down low in the solar plexus, this type of blow is called a Rabbit Punch in boxing. Boxers frown on it and get bent out of shape if you do it while sparring. The reason is that it's too effective (so take a hint).

IMPACT AREA

Phoenix

The next booger you should know about is called a Phoenix Punch. It's not something you want to throw a N.N.B.R. with, unless you're into broken fingers. It should be kept at the Setup and Rattler levels. (Don't worry, though, because it's ugly enough right where it is.)

The obvious use of the Phoenix is to land in the tender spots where a fist can't go with such accuracy. You get pegged

Phoenix Punch.

in the arm/chest joint and you're going to know about this one. The flip side of this is if you try to peg someone on their forehead with this one, you're going to know the definition of a broken finger. The problem with this blow, aside from its having to be accurate, is that it takes a moment to get your hand into position. That's why you should use it when a fight has boiled down to shuffling around and throwing jabs and punches (as fights occasionally do). If the guy is crawling all over you, you may not have the opportunity to shift your hand into the right position for this one.

Karate Chop

Next is the world-famous Karate Chop, referred to by those in the know as a "Knife Hand." It's a useful little blow—low mileage, okay maintenance, and used by a little old sensei to go to the dojo on Sundays.

One thing about this one that folks don't talk too much about is that you can use either the pinky or

IMPACT AREA

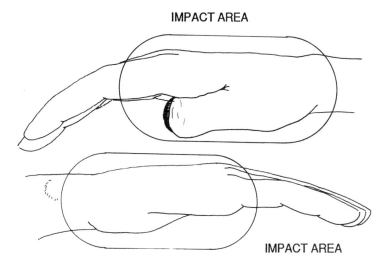

IMPACT AREA

Knife Hand, or bent-finger karate chops, thumb and knife sides.

thumb side of the hand. A bit of advice, however: if you're going to use the thumb side, tuck your thumb under the flat of your palm. (It doesn't get crushed that way.) One of my favorite strikes when a guy throws a N.N.B.R. at me (for openers) is to block while sidestepping into his now-exposed side area. If you can do it (which I can), grab the guy's punching arm with your front (blocking) arm. Then, with your rear hand in a knife position, sweep up the length of his now-trapped arm. The target is his throat, but you can break a nose this way as well. The striking area is the thumb side. It's scary how many people will fall for this.

Another thing that amazes me is the number of people who try to do this with their fingers held straight out. Don't ask me why, but somehow the fingers are stronger when they are bent. If you try a Knife Hand with straight fingers, you're just begging for a hand cast. To tell the truth it's even easier to use the hand position used for a Leopard/Bear Swat than to risk your fingers.

Other Strikes

Moving on now to strikes that utilize other parts of the anatomy to make life really uncomfortable for the unsuspecting, let's take two of my favorites—the elbows and the knees.

Elbow Shots

Part of what makes an elbow shot effective is that it uses the body. In other words, a good elbow shot comes from the hips. Most Americanized styles don't teach elbow shots because they're not allowed in the ring . . . er . . . mat. Oddly enough, in Muay Thai (Thai kickboxing) they are, and the word is wicked. This kind of shot can be used as a N.N.B.R. because the elbow has the structure to take the punishment.

Elbows can be used in two ways. One is where the arm alone moves quickly and stops somewhere around the guy's guts or face. These hurt, but they aren't especially harmful. The real danger is when someone puts all of his body weight behind the elbow. You can do this by twisting the torso or stepping in a particular direction. Play around with it and you'll figure it out.

Knee Strikes

Combatants misuse knees often. I've been kneed inefficiently before, and it made for a rather interesting situation. His thigh went between my legs, and I sort of sat on it as it rode upward. Yes, it picked me up about two inches off the ground, but it didn't do any damage. It felt like I was riding a pony. Yipee kiyaah!

The problem with the way most people use knees is the same one most people have with the way they punch. Instead of hitting, they try to push *through* their target. A proper blow should only go about two inches into your opponent. That means it goes full speed and stops two inches in. It doesn't mean it begins to slow down before it hits and then coasts to a stop two inches in. Nor does it mean that it's aimed six inches in and only gets in two inches before it stops. The blow simply stops two inches in. It could go in further, but it doesn't. It stops where you want it to, not where it runs out of steam. This transfers all the energy of the blow into your opponent, which makes it an effective punch. When you throw all your weight in an unbalanced manner and the energy is interrupted because you're targeting six inches behind his head, this is *not* an effective punch.

It's the same way with knees. When you swing your knee, its target is inside the guy's body, not wherever the energy poops out. Using this formula, the knees become a more useful part of your arsenal because you can use them to effectively damage something besides his nuts.

• • • • •

Okay, I've just about shot my wad about blows, but there are two more little things I want to add to this chapter.

Number one is that it doesn't matter if it's a punch or a kick, the law is the same: *get out as fast as you went in!* No shit, folks. This is especially true if you're up against a guy who is bigger and stronger than you are. He can damage you more, so you have to avoid being caught. If the guy you're fighting gets his hands on you, unless you know how to street wrestle, nine times out of ten the outcome is going to be decided by size. Also, when you're up against a trained fighter and you leave anything hanging out, he's going to break it. No lie.

Number two is a streetfighting law, and it sends martial artists up the wall. Tough, it's true. *Never kick above your waist or turn your back on an opponent while kicking!* You can turn your back on your opponent when you're in the process of running like hell. Do not, however, kick above the waist in a streetfight. This is the best way to get your nuts ripped off that has ever come down the pikeway.

In this chapter, I have covered the basic blows that I'm going to be talking about. I have also covered many of the basics of blows that should help you out. In my first book, *Cheap Shots*, I covered a lot more territory. In this one I'll be more specific. I advise you to read my first book to get a broader picture of what else is involved in fighting.

Now, on to a thing of equal importance: how not to get hurt too badly by this very stuff.

CHAPTER TWO

Shedding

Winning a fight is a two-part process. One is inflicting the most damage to the other guy; two is minimizing the amount of damage you take.

—From a conversation with a boxer

In *Cheap Shots* I spoke of mobility as a way to save your ass. It's still true. Don't get hit if you can avoid it. If, however, you have the misfortune to be on the receiving end of a blow, there are things you can do.

When you're done reading this book, you'll know what you really want to protect. I will gladly take a blow to the jaw rather than the throat. I can keep on fighting with a fractured jaw; a collapsed windpipe not only makes fighting difficult, it can also foul up your attempts at living. In the same way, if I see something coming at my collarbone, I'll roll out of the way and take it on the chest. My chest can take it, my collarbone can't.

This awareness is used in combination with intensified blocking attempts and a thing called "shedding." Shedding is from boxing, and it's part of the reason that boxers are such sons of bitches to tangle with. It can be summed up best by a reaction I once heard to it: "If I could ever land a solid punch on him, I'd hurt him bad." It's a technique used to prevent a blow from landing solidly, and it's accomplished by moving slightly. You're still going to get hit, but you minimize the damage it does by changing the angle of impact. It really doesn't sound like much, but it is.

Boxing shedding is slightly modified for our purposes because there are certain angles of attack that

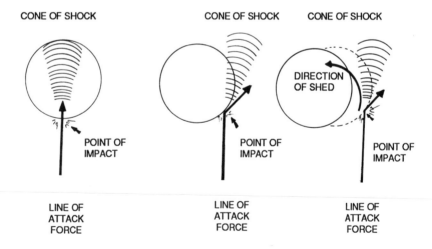

Three balls with lines of impact directly centered (left), off-center with impact ricocheting off (center), and off-center with impact causing ball to spin the other way (right).

don't exist in the ring but do in the street. The idea, however, is definitely the same. The first thing we're going to do is look at our balls.

The first ball might as well be a cube because all of the energy is going into it. This means it absorbs all of the damaging impact. This is the equivalent of "taking a punch" (a legendary stupidity).

The second ball uses its natural shape to deflect the energy of the impact, which decreases the amount of energy actually delivered to the ball. The energy still exists, but it's going off in a harmless direction. This is why towers on castles were round. It deflected the impact of a catapulted rock so the tower didn't have to take the whole mess. This is also something that— believe it or not—we have built into us. Your head, in case you hadn't noticed, is round. The same physical principles can be applied to deflect blows from your face.

The third ball is the really special one. Unlike the first two, it's smart enough not to sit there and take the impact. By adding mobility to its already good shape, it minimizes the damage it receives. The energy pushes it aside, but the full brunt is not delivered. In effect, this makes all of the energy harmless. If you've ever played pool, you know what happens when you hit the cue ball far enough off center. It goes spinning off about six inches to the side and stops, while you fall face-first onto the pool table and all your friends laugh. (Like it's never happened to them. Yeah, sure.) That is the best example of what shedding is about—deflecting the energy of a blow by using mobility as well as natural shape.

This is not something you're going to be able to go out and do right off the bat. It's going to take some serious practice with your sparring partner(s), and it's going to take some research. Go out and find information about boxing at a gym or in books, and start practicing it. Shedding is something your body is going to need to know how to do. It's a fast and subtle technique that you have to train your body to do instinctively. In time, your mind will have very little to do with the process. Some guy will throw a punch and, faster than your mind can think, your body will shift to minimize the damage. If you've ever heard the expression "roll with the punches," you now know what it means. That's what being a good fighter is about.

You can use the same technique with the rest of your body and in different directions. If you "see" a punch coming at one of your vital areas, you can begin to roll out of the way. In the Oriental styles, there's an imaginary string that runs down the middle of the body. If pressure is applied to the left side of the body, the string becomes the axis that the rest of the body spins around. Try to imagine that string as you're learning this. If you have trouble with that one, a metal rod that runs through your body and plants into the ground might work as an image. Either way, it works.

Try to avoid taking the entire impact of any blow thrown at you. There are fighting styles that are based on avoiding your opponent's direct energy and using it against him at the same time. Tai chi, aikido, and, of course, judo are called the "soft styles." They rely on moving out of the way of an attack and then using that same energy against the attacker. The main reason these styles work against people, by the way, is that the attacker is off balance nine times out of ten. Most people try to throw a N.N.B.R. as their opening move. This is basically unwise, because at the opening of a fight, when everybody is fresh, the odds are against the blow landing. Also, since most people don't know how to stay in balance during such an attack, they leave themselves wide open to the old "chuck him on his head" move.

Again, there are certain angles that aren't covered by boxing-type shedding. Overhead punches are kind of rare in the ring. They do happen, but not to the extreme that I'm talking about. I've never seen a Hanging Punch in a boxing match, and since Palm Strikes, a.k.a. Rabbit Punches, are a bozo no-no anyway, you don't see punches coming in from above much. The way to avoid these mothers is to simply lean back or twist aside. If the blow is heading toward your face, you may want to tuck your chin into your chest when you do it. This way, you allow the blow to roll down off you while protecting your tender spots.

Shedding and mobility should be considered your second line of defense. If somebody lets fly with a roundhouse kick that gets past your defenses for some reason, what should you do? Tighten up and take it? Nah, just move with it. The way the blow is heading is the direction in which you should start moving. This will decrease the impact you'll receive. By the way, I think a roundhouse kick is one of the most overused (and therefore useless) kicks around. It's easy to block and, because it's taught so widely, everybody expects one. Other things would work better, but people have been taught to throw a roundhouse as the general kick, and so they do, regardless of whether it works or not.

A little bit of physics here, folks. You'll notice that in the illustrations of blocks on the next page, block B isn't moving in the first one. That means when block A hits, block B is going to receive a 50 MPH impact. Yet, look at the next one. Since block B is moving at 30 MPH, that means the actual impact it's going to receive is lessened. In fact it's only going to take about 20 MPH-worth of impact. The same thing applies to

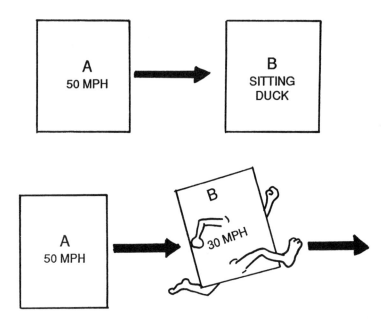

Because block B isn't moving in the top illustration, it's going to receive a 50 MPH impact when block A hits. But in the bottom illustration, block B is moving at 30 MPH, so the actual impact from block A will be less (about 20 MPH).

punches and kicks. You can withstand the reduced impact better than you can take the whole enchilada. So move!

Most people don't know the stuff in this book, which could make their lives easier (in a sense). For the most part, people won't be targeting the vital points of your body intentionally. They may find them accidentally, but them's the odds. Learning to protect these spots by getting them out of the way, as well as by blocking, will improve your chances. This is important, because most of those "I gave him my best shot and he just looked at me" stories are based on the fact that nothing vital was hit. Once you know how frail the human body actually is, you'll want to start covering your own dick.

Another thing I want you to think about. Now that you know how to lessen the damage of a blow, you also know what someone else can do, intentionally or not, to lessen the effectiveness of *your* blows. The poor technique most people demonstrate when hitting (out of balance, loose muscles, incorrect physics), combined with the the fact that most targets are moving (shedding), seriously reduces the effectiveness of a number of moves. The way to yield results from these target areas is to *practice*! These new and improved target areas ain't going to do shit for you if you don't improve the physics of your strikes. Targeting is another thing you need to practice. When you throw in the necessary speed, your targeting can get a little twitchy if you haven't practiced.

Basically, what I'm trying to say is that you shouldn't rely on any one of these targets to do all the work for you. Their effectiveness lies in the sum total of damage done, not just one strike. I know that's a little more scary, but wars are won the same way. It's not one battle that wins a war, but a collective tab.

I'm saying this stuff from the point of view of a streetfighter. There's a world of difference between the street and the mat. Part of the difference is—and I hate to say it—that the mat is a business. You don't sell stuff by telling unpleasant truths. You sell by giving guarantees, even false ones. I, on the other hand, have nothing to lose by telling the truth. What I have to gain by telling the truth is the knowledge that I may save your ass one day.

So again, I stress: don't rely on any one of these things to do all of your work for you. You gotta keep his bill higher than yours. That's the way to win.

CHAPTER THREE

The Noggin

Those who know how to win are far more numerous than those who know how to make proper use of their victories.

—Polybius

The head. It can be hard, it can be screwed on tight, it can be given, it can be used, or it can be knocked off. One of the things that amazes me to this day is the number of people who randomly throw punches to the face, expecting them to do something.

Blows to the face do have psychological impact. This is why Setups to the face are so good. They freak the guy out. Now the truth is, a freakout is good, but it isn't damage.

Let's take a look at the human skull.

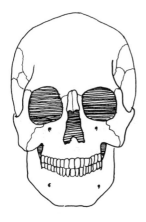 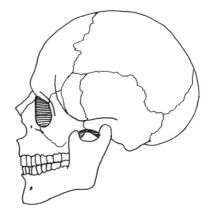

Front and side view of skull.

Ugly mother, ain't it? There is something you should notice about it, though. *It's made of fuckin' bone! It's hard!* It's the most condensed package of bone in the human body! The hip is bigger, but it spreads out. Face it, this hunk of bone carries the brain and the second strongest muscle in the body, the jaw. It's well armored! A sloppy punch to the face ain't going to do shit, damagewise. To do real damage to the head and face, you either need to use massive impact (N.N.B.R.) or target chinks in the armor. A small advantage is that although some of the chinks don't really cause too much damage, they do cause pain sensors to go batshit.

The temple is one such puppy. Believe it or not, it's surrounded by the thickest part of the skull. Yet, because of nerves around that neck of the woods, getting knocked upside the temple hurts like a bitch. If you have assassin's fingers (able to punch through wood), the temple might work as a target. Other than that, it's more painful than damageable

Wait a minute, I just thought of something I should

explain here. The infamous "knockout." Officially, a concussion is just getting knocked out. However, they don't really worry about it until it gets more serious. A knockout is the result of a rather bizarre set of circumstances. See, the brain actually floats in a liquid casing inside your skull. This stuff is rather thick and doesn't compress or slosh around too much, sort of like brake fluid. This keeps your bean from actually touching the walls of your skull. Your brain can do all sorts of neat things, but it can't stand being bounced off the brainpan walls. When you're knocked out (most times), what has happened is that you have received enough of an impact to cause your brain to touch the walls. Bamo! The lights go out. How hard it connects determines how long you're out, how much damage you've received, and if you're ever going to wake up again.

The brain is not designed to be drop-kicked across the room. It's actually a very delicate organ. If you get slammed hard upside the head, the area where the brain hits is going to be damaged. When I was doing drugs, one of the jokes we had was based on some very careful phrasing from the scientific community, which states that "nearly three-quarters of the human brain is not used." We thought that meant that we had brain cells to burn.

The truth of the matter is that scientists don't know what three-quarters of the brain *does*. Their careful phrasing covers the fact that they don't know what the fuck is going on. With all their fancy words and pompous posturing it eventually boils down to the fact that they don't know how the brain works. Actually, that three-quarters is very important, and if it's damaged you're in some deep shit.

Different parts of the brain affect different parts of the whole. For example, Broca's area is in the front part of the brain that sits over your eyes. It controls speech. If it's damaged, you can't talk any more. You can understand, but the software program for responding is shot to hell. The tongue and vocal cords still work, but the orders are messed up.

The real bitch about concussions is that the damage doesn't always show up immediately. Blackouts can begin weeks later. Numbness can occur in parts of the body that are controlled by the damaged part. Loss of motor and nerve control often results from head injury. All sorts of nasty shit can happen from getting knocked out, and it isn't something that goes away inside of a week. It can take years to go away, if ever.

This is why grabbing a club to hit somebody when you're pissed isn't a good idea. If you fuck someone up, there's a good chance that someone else is going to get annoyed about it. If it can be done to others, it can be done to you. That's the street. The cops are another story altogether. They call this stuff all sorts of nasty names, like "attempted murder," "aggravated assault," and my favorite, "assault with a deadly weapon."

If, however, the guy had the poor taste to jump out of the bushes and attack you, leave him where he falls. Don't even call the cops. (By the way, legally speaking, I didn't say that. It's a joke, ha ha! The law says you have to report this sort of thing, but when they try to throw your ass in jail, you'll understand why I just made that joke.) Unless your breath is clean, people are going to be interested in finding out why you beat the dirtbag up.

Back to how the brain works. It appears that different people are literally wired differently. There's a study going on that's based on the theory that different quarters of the brain do different things. What's more, different quarters are dominant in different people. That means how you think and how your brain works are not the same as the guy standing next to you.

There are four quadrants of the brain, and each is in charge of different operations. Left rear is data and information. Left front is analytical thinking, logic, and reason. Right front is imagination and visual imaging (like artists do). Right rear is in charge of basic or primitive emotions (such as the old fight-or-flight mechanism).

You can avoid a lot of fights by realizing that the other guy isn't intentionally being an asshole by not seeing something your way. A sizable hunk of the time the guy literally can't understand what your point is. It's not that he's stupid, it's just that his brain operates along totally different lines. There's no right or wrong way to think. In specific situations there are *better* ways to think, but there is no overall "right" way. Often, what works in one situation is totally wrong for another. A whole shitload of trouble happens when one system tries to cram its way down the throats of other systems. The way around this is to watch how people with different dominant quadrants operate. Also, start paying attention to the different quadrants within yourself and how they work. This will allow you to shift gears and deal with people on their own terms. You can avoid a whole lot of shit by being able to communicate with people in their own system. When it's over, you can shift back to the way you normally think. The actual goal is to get through life without too many hassles. While you may have to bounce somebody off the wall occasionally, you'll get along much easier if you can keep it to a minimum.

By the way, our school system was designed by people who fell over backwards to the left. Rote memorization and data retrieval are all left-rear brain functions. If you didn't do too well with memorizing or you feel bad about the trouble you had in school, don't. Face it, our educational system was designed in such a way that, at best, only one in four people would feel at home. Trying to force one system's dominance over others leads to all sorts of trouble.

There's a lot of twisted, fucked up people out there who are the victims of this very thing. The real bitch about this is that they don't strike back at the people who actually hurt them. They come over and take their crazies out on people like you. The other thing they do is go after people who look like the person who hurt them. The proof of this is that an ungodly percentage of rapes are against women over fifty. One in four women will be raped during their lives, and many of them will be past the age of thirty when it happens.

To be truly good at self-defense, you need to know how to technically defend yourself against physical attacks, but you also need to know about people. If you understand that people's minds work differently, you can maneuver within the various systems and keep from putting yourself into situations where you'll have to use violence. Until you get good at avoiding problems, though, you'd better be able to kick some ass.

Above the Ear

Back to the head and which areas are most vulnerable to damage. While the temple hurts, the forehead is basically a waste of time as a target. It's got the structural support to take all sorts of abuse. Over the ear, however, is a painful spot. If it is hit hard enough the brain will ricochet off the skull. Poke around there with a light Phoenix and find the place that hurts the most. That's your target. The reason it's a little more effective than coming in from the face is that there is less bone to absorb the impact before the brain gets involved.

The Base of the Skull

The base of the skull has great jamming potential. It has to do with the fact that the spinal cord enters at this point. A solid N.N.B.R. may not knock the guy out cold, but it'll overload his circuits for a sizable chunk of time. (Remember, most boxing knockouts aren't total unconsciousness. The guy is rolling around on the floor trying to get up. This is still a knockout.) A Bear Swat, a Hanging Punch, an elbow strike—all the heavy-impact blows will slow someone down when delivered to the base of the skull. It may not stop them, but it'll hurt them.

The best way to avoid these head shots is to shed. If someone comes at you with an overhand club shot, shed it to the side and take it on the shoulder. A sideswipe can and should be avoided by ducking or backpedaling out of the way. Whatever you do, don't take these mothers. They are dangerous.

The Face

Okay, the face. Unless you're a real knuckle-dragger who can cave in walls with a single blow, the cheeks and forehead are out as damageable targets. This doesn't mean you shouldn't toss in a few Rattlers and Setups to those parts of the face. Just know that what you're doing is psyching the guy out rather than really hurting him. It's a mindfuck to get pegged in the face. It flusters you and screws up your confidence.

This is why open sparring is so important. Get together with some friends. Start out slow (maybe with open-hand slap boxing) and work your way up. At first, you're gonna be all hairless about getting hit in the face, but after a while it becomes only mildly annoying. Then, after a bit more, it's going to become second nature to shed and duck. This is really important. You have to learn not to be terrified of getting hit. It's not fun to get pegged, but when you've experienced it in enough sparring matches, it's no longer a freakout. When you don't freak out, you can stay calm in a fight. When you stay calm in a fight, winning becomes a regular occurrence.

Along the same lines, while straight punches to the forehead and cheeks are mostly ruled out as far as potential damage is concerned, that doesn't mean you can't strike these areas with heavier blows. You can really jingle somebody's noggin with one of the palm-type hits. A Bear Swat, Dragon, or Palm Strike can make people's brains wiggle. This is a more advanced form of psych-out than a plain-old Rattler. While it will drop the guy occasionally, don't bet your dick on it. You have a better chance of dropping the guy from a side blow than you do from the front.

The Schnozz

Let's look at the old snot locker a minute. Nine out of ten people will definitely not want to play any more if you bust their nose. A busted nose hurts all the way down to your stomach. If you're like me, you feel like you're getting ready to throw up (which I do, after I stomp the guy for hurting me so badly). If you've ever had a busted nose from a baseball, or running into a wall, or some childhood (emphasis on the "hood" part) mishap, you know what I'm talking about.

In case you didn't know, the nose really isn't bone, it's cartilage (the same stuff that makes your ear stiff).

Cartilage is flexible and less likely to break. It is, however, anchored to bone. Most times, a busted nose consists of the nose cartilage (septum) upping anchor and trying to sail south for the winter.

The first time is the worst (ow, pain, hurt, whimper. . .) because all of the connections are still there. Afterwards, many of the mooring lines don't reconnect, or they reconnect but not as strongly. This means it's easier to get a broken nose after you've already had one. So while the cartilage seldom actually gets broken, it does get broken loose.

One small detail you should consider is that a broken nose hurts the other guy less the second time, too. Not that it doesn't put a searing pain through his head—it does. But because the nose is broken again there is less actual damage done this time. More scary is that it's a familiar pain. That means it's less likely to stop the guy dead in his tracks. Eeek!

Let's look at how the schnozzola is connected to the skull. The part that binds the cartilage to the skull is farther back than where you usually find your finger. It's also higher up. Reach up and grab where your nose runs into your eyes. That's bone. In fact, these are the nasal bones. Now move down a bit. Where your fingers suddenly slide off something hard and pinch together is where the cartilage begins. Now, what is the most likely approach vector to get to this mooring?

If you said "from higher up," give yourself a cookie. (We'll deal with the myth of low shots planting noses in the brain later.) It's odd, but most people who swing at someone's nose actually aim too low to do any real damage. It you take a hit with the guy's knuckle on the level of the tip of your nose, all it's going to do is take the flexible cartilage and bend it over. While it is possible to break someone's nose by hitting here, the physics are incredibly difficult. The speed of the striking object has to be faster than the flexing speed of the cartilage.

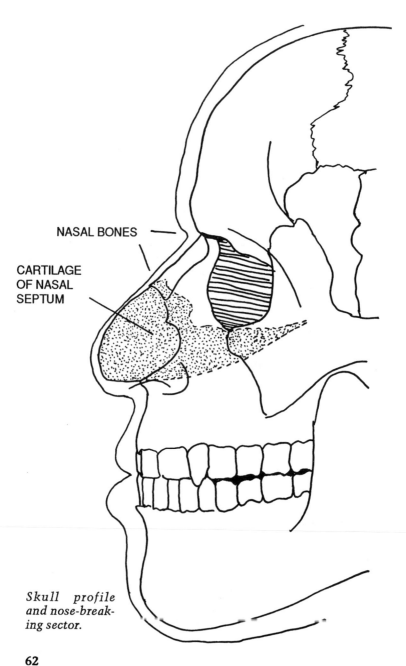

NASAL BONES

CARTILAGE
OF NASAL
SEPTUM

*Skull profile
and nose-break-
ing sector.*

A baseball might be fast enough, but unless the guy's a kung fu expert, the odds are seriously against it happening from a fist.

However, if you take that same amount of impact and bring it into play three inches higher, it's a different story. A straight-on shot might pop the moorings loose, but a hook with the knuckles can really blow it loose.

Let's look at some of those overhead swats and hangers. Because of the way the nose is connected, it really isn't designed to take too much pressure coming in from above (more so, because it's the most exposed from that angle). Hitting the top of the nose with a downward strike is a god-awful nasty blow. Do it right and you'll knock the guy's nose onto his chest. Do it wrong and you'll bounce off his brow and just sort of mush his nose where it is (if you don't miss it all together).

If you look at the illustration you'll see the profile of the skull. The shaded shape is the septum (the cartilage part). Look how deep that sucker is anchored at the bottom! On top, however, the septum is anchored to the two parallel nasal bones that make up the ridge of your nose. These suckers can be broken (actually, smashed is a better description). While the swats and hangers are your best bet, the ridge of the nose is one of the few straight-shot possibilities in the entire head. Whatever you use, if you break these it's N.N.B.R. time. Nine times out of ten, the fight's going to be over.

Okay, I don't mind myths as long as they have something to do with reality. For instance, I did not do a diving, forward roll and put four rounds from a .38 into a water truck. That's the legend. I did, however, charge and play chicken with a one-ton pickup truck. I had a spear, he had a truck. It was even. He stopped, not because he was afraid of hurting me, but because it was a company truck. He didn't want to explain a spear through the radiator to his boss. That's the truth.

There's a legend that I really don't like. It's one of those "guaranteed moves" legends. Everyone knows about it, and yet, nobody has actually tried it. *But they'll still tell you about it!* It's the upper shot to the nose. Yes indeed, I'm talking about driving the guy's nose bone into his brain! In a blaze of glorious kung fueyness, you'll kill your attacker in one swift, deadly move. (Excuse me, I'm going to be sick.)

Now, based on what I've just explained to you, what's wrong with the idea of driving the guy's nose bone into his brain? Yeah—there ain't no bone in the nose. Also, if you look at the illustration, you'll see that there *is* bone *between* your boogers and your brains.

If you look very closely at the illustration, you will see that there are two tiny, itsy-bitsy, teeny-weeny little holes in the skull leading from the eye sockets into the

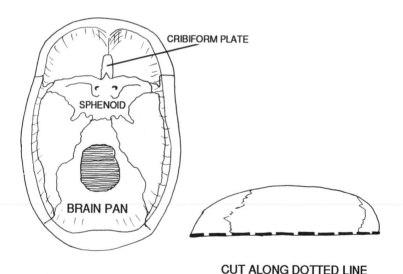

Bottom view of skull.

brain cavity. Unfortunately for would-be Bruce Lees, while your victim is alive, these are stuffed with nerves, which makes it real hard for splintered nose bones to travel through them and embed themselves into the brain. The actual theory behind this is that if you hit the nose fast and hard enough, the blow bypasses crushing the cartilage (which would slow it down) and proceeds to cause a chain reaction of impacts that eventually ends up with the cribiform plate snapping the cleats that anchor it in place and then slipping up and separating the lobes of the brain. Face it, you've got as good a chance of doing someone this way as you do of the government lowering taxes. (In other words, "possible, but not fucking likely.")

This whole myth originated a few thousand years back. In China, the golden age of martial arts occurred before somebody realized they could do something more with gunpowder than make firecrackers. Legends of superhuman feats abound from that period. (In fact, most of the "superman kung fu" flicks are supposed to have happened during that time.) Thing is, these guys did nothing but practice. I'm talking about doing the same move 100,000 times. Learning a full set could run you twenty years. With that much practice, these guys could crush skulls with one punch.

With this sort of dedication and practice, these people discovered all sorts of stuff about the human body and its potential that still puts science on its ass. Chi kung (or qi gong, chee kong, depending on dialect and translator) is an internal discipline that literally turns your body into iron. I mean a human tank, where you get a chair busted across your back and you turn and look at the guy. Western scientists and doctors say this sort of stuff is impossible. (They also say that faster-than-light travel is impossible, a claim that I disproved personally when a burglar tried to bury a hatchet in my head. I scared the shit out of the guy, because nobody is supposed to be able to move that fast. Of course, it didn't do my sphincter any good, either.)

Anyway, it was during the Incredible Hulk time of kung fu that this nose-picking technique was used. Even then, though, it was an execution reserved for the emperor's court. That means the guy had been sentenced to death, was tied up and couldn't move.

Having played with human skulls in my time, I can tell you a thing or two about them. If you ever meet me and are confused by a guy named Animal being so kicked back, let me tell you a story of my wayward youth. We used to have a human skull, whose name I forget. Anyway, we had heard that the Vikings used to make goblets out of the skulls of their enemies. With that in mind, we started guzzling beer out of the skull. It was great. I'd walk up to strange women and say, "How about a little head?" As they'd be winding up for a bout of indignity that would make Mount St. Helens look like a burp, I'd hold up the skull. As they flipped out, I'd laugh and take a drink. They'd go bye-bye when I did that. God, I'm lucky I didn't get arrested . . . but, I digress.

As I was saying, having held a skull or two I can tell you that the thinnest, most delicate part of the brain case is over the eye. A blow from one of the ancients, even if it didn't break the cribiform plate loose, smashing it into the brain, would have smashed enough of the seams to drain the sinuses real quick. Also, the brain-packing juice would have dribbled out. So if you've got twenty years and the inclination to do something 100,000 times, you too can qualify for the job of Chinese Imperial Executioner.

Sorry if I popped anyone's bubble about that one. (Actually, no I'm not. I despise garbage espoused as gospel.) The fact that you can't be a kung fu killer

shouldn't prevent you from knowing about the underside of the nose. Upward pressure on the nose is
extremely painful. I suspect that's where the myth got
its roots (sort of like me and the spear that escalated to
a .38—it sounds more impressive that way).

So the bottom of the nose is not out as a target. Far
from it. An uppercut can and will bust someone's nose
loose from the moorings. Even if it doesn't, it hurts like
a bitch. In a wrestling match or grappling situation,
you can move someone out of your way very quickly.
Open your hand with your thumb out from your palm,
slap your hand over the guys upper jaw, with his nose
in the "V" formed by your hand and thumb. Now, lift
and put upward pressure on the bottom of his nose.
Moses didn't get as fast a parting as you'll get. Try it on
yourself and see how much it smarts.

The same trick can be done with just one finger, but
I prefer the way I just told you because it's harder to
shake off. It's just a diversionary technique, however.
You do it while you're either trying to get away or as
you're winding up to slug the guy a good one. If you
stick around too long he might just figure out that he
can bite the shit out of you. A thumb up the nostril is
also an effective way to make people wiggle their
heads trying to get away. But again, these are devices
designed to give you time to do something else.

The Eyes

Let's move to the eyes for a minute. In case you
hadn't noticed, eyes are sort of squishy. Unfortunately,
this makes them nearly useless as large-striking-surface
targets. A punch to the eye may cause a flash and
hurt, but it ain't going to do too much damage. It'll
swell up into a black eye, it's true. Unfortunately, that
takes time. It's gotta take at least three or four serious

Rattlers before there's even a remote chance of its swelling closed. (The odds are seriously against this happening during the actual fight.)

Again, this does not mean the eyes should be disregarded as targets. The clawing techniques are primo here. The eyes are susceptible to clawing, gouging, poking, and other unpleasantries. Corkscrewing your thumb into somebody's eye during a fight can convince them that they really don't want to be where they are at the moment.

The most effective way to punch the eyes is to

IMPACT AREA

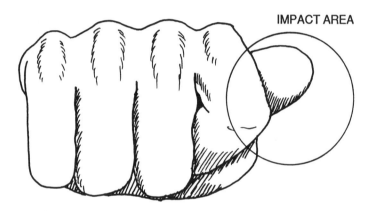

Thumb hook (eyes as target sector).

extend the thumb. As your index knuckle smashes into the nose, your thumb gouges into the eye. This is called a thumb hook, and it's another bozo no-no in the boxing ring. Check out the illustration and you'll see how to do it effectively. This is one of those moves that will usually end a fight, namely because it hurts like a bitch and temporarily blinds the guy. (I don't advise it unless it's a really serious situation, like the guy has been gunning for you and has you cornered in an alley with five dudes backing him up. If your thumb nail is long, you can slash his eye open. But anytime somebody goes to the hospital they can drag you up on attempted murder or assault charges, so be real careful about using this stuff.)

People get kind of wigged out about things coming at their eyes, which is why a slash at the eyes during a knife fight is another one of the best ways to convince the guy that he really doesn't want to be there. It's mostly psychological, as are most blows to the eyes.

There's one more trick I might mention here. It has to do with rings. I'm not really hot about punch rings, for reasons I explained in another book. Some of them are nasty little beasts designed for gouging eyes and tearing flesh; their use is obvious. However, if you're wearing a ring that isn't an eye-gouger, you can still use it against the eyes, but in a roundabout way. If you aim at the eyebrows with a fast Setup, you can sometimes break the skin. Blood in the eye not only stings, it hinders vision. You know how much you bleed when you cut yourself shaving; use that to your advantage for a change.

The Ears

Okay, ears. In case you haven't noticed, there's very little lethal damage that can be done via the ear. (Okay, so Hamlet's old man was taken out by poison in the ear. But if it were really that effective, anyone who watches "The Lawrence Welk Show" would have been dead a long time ago.) This does not mean that the ears are not useful. If you grab a handful of ear and jerk downward along the side of the head, the results can be interesting.

The ear is made out of cartilage and flesh; it contains no bone and few nerve endings. So basically, it's useless as a target for anything other than being torn off. You go for an ear rip and the guy might decide that messing with you is not such a hot idea, 'cause he's going to start worrying about what you're going to try to rip off next. The drawback of going for an ear, however, is that he may decide it's combat, and then it's going to get ugly. Therefore, you should consider both timing and the mental makeup of the opponent before you go trying to pull his ear off.

Another fun trick is to insert a finger into his ear and pull. This isn't terribly effective unless you use the palm of your other hand (on the other side of his head) to pin him into a position that keeps him from jerking his head away from your finger in his ear. Yep, you can move someone out of your way right quick with just one finger. Don't try and overuse this move though. It's more of a one-time surprise to get the guy out of the way. You move him and then either do something else to hold him still or start hitting him somewhere else.

Something I've heard about but have never seen or encountered is the cupped slap to the ear used to pop the eardrum. It's physically possible but contingent on a few factors. One is whether the guy's mouth is closed or not. Since you're basically relying on the same physics that a concussion from an explosion uses to blow out someone's eardrum, the conditions have to be the same. See, the ear ducts connect down in the throat. If the mouth is closed, there is no chance of the pressure equalizing. If, however, the guy's mouth is open, the same pressure-equalizing system that makes your ears pop comes into play. (That's why you open your mouth around an explosion.)

The other condition that has to be met is that you hit correctly. You cup your hand and hit flat against the head with the rim of that cup. It's the compression of air that does the damage. The air looks for an out and either escapes through any holes or blows out the weakest point of the eardrum and escapes that way. If your hand isn't held so enough air is compressed, or if the air escapes through an opening left by one side of your hand, the blow won't work. These are difficult circumstances to replicate, which is why I've never actually seen this one done. (That doesn't mean it can't be done, though, so don't get careless about slaps.) While I've never had my eardrums blown, I have had my chimes rung pretty well by slaps.

By the way, the difference between a slap and one of the swats that I've told you about is that slaps are done with loose hands. With slaps, the wrist reaches a certain stress point and begins to fold back. This means the amount of energy being delivered is only as great as the wrist's resistance point. Swats are tightened down so the full force of the blow is delivered. I speak from experience when I say there's a big difference between getting slapped and getting swatted. I've been slapped more than I've been swatted. (The reasons that I got slapped are just between me and the hers.)

Incidentally, I don't agree with hitting women. If you often find yourself so mad at somebody that you want to hit them, *walk away*. I mean leave. You don't have to be in that sort of relationship. There is a program inside of the human male that keeps him from attacking women. Men also have programs that lean them toward aggression, and the proper use of these is to *protect* women and children. We're the ones that are supposed to stop the attacks against the tribe.

The problem occurs when the safety stops are removed. This can be the result of training or trauma. If, because of an emotionally traumatic experience or consistent negative enforcement, these safety stops are overridden, you end up with rapists, wife beaters, and child abusers.

So if you find yourself regularly getting so pissed at someone that you want to strike them, *get the fuck out of the situation.* It is the road to Hell. Those dirtbags out there that attack other people have lost the safety stops. They are the mad dogs; some can be brought back, but most need to be exterminated. The thing is, if you aren't careful the same can happen to you. That's why it's important to know other aspects of self-defense—the information that will keep you from blowing a gasket and going mad-dog.

When it comes to targeting, the area just below the ear and behind the jaw is another story. Yes indeed, getting hit here can make your nuts fall off and go rolling around the floor. It does little actual physical damage, but then again, neither does someone hitting your dick with a hammer. This does not mean it's a pleasant experience. It is one of the little flukes of human anatomy that this critical point is just sort of flapping in the wind. A well-placed Phoenix Punch to this area will slow down even the biggest gorilla. It jams the system long enough for you to get in two or three more good licks before the guy can recover. This target is really good for convincing people that they don't want to fight you. If you hit somebody here, though, and they shrug it off or just get mad, you are in a heap of shit. It's basically the equivalent of getting kicked in the nuts.

This is a key target area for street wrestlers. If you end up in a grapple with somebody and they try to grind a thumb into you at this point, a quick jerk of your head is in order. I know it's kind of hard to remember at that precise moment, but since you're moving your head anyway, you might consider trying to dent his nose with your forehead.

The Jaw

The jaw is one of those areas that people seem to assume is a primo target just because it's there. I have been pegged in the jaw more times than I can remember, and I have to say that unless you hit it right, or the other guy is doing something wildly wrong, it's a waste of time for doing serious damage.

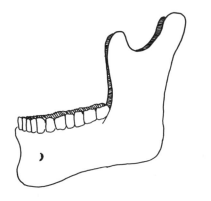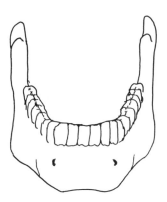

The human jaw bone.

Let's look at a human jaw. Notice anything solid about it? Yeah, it's one solid hunk of bone! What's more, it's shaped like an A-frame. Just in case two plus two ain't equalled four yet, realize that the mother is held in place by both tendon and one of the strongest muscles in the human body. To make it a further giggle, when people are pissed, it's natural physiological reaction to lock their jaw muscle. Go ahead, hit somebody on the jaw. The way most people throw punches, it's a wonder they don't break their hands more often. Unless you can throw a mothering fast N.N.B.R. every time, the jaw is sort of limited as a target.

Well, hell, there goes everything that you've

learned from Chuck Norris movies. Think back to all the times you've been socked in the jaw. If you were caught flat-footed, it might have done some damage. Aside from hurting like a mother, it might have jolted the tendons because you didn't have your jaw clamped. During a fight, it might have hurt when you got pegged and later clicked when you were rubbing it, wondering why you had gotten into a fight afterall. It stayed sore for a couple of days, but basically, no real damage done.

Okay, now we get into the real hairy part. Let's say the gorilla you're up against is a boxer. He's got an ugly gift called a hook that he's just achin' to give to you. Some of the broken jaws that I've encountered have come from hooks. This is because the jaw is only designed to work in an up-and-down motion. (While it can do it, side-to-side isn't its strongest suit.) Most often, those little flanges that sit against the skull get busted. Occasionally, if the guy is real good, he can shatter the jaw just before it turns upward. Fortunately, this kind of pro is rare (thank God).

If you can throw a N.N.B.R. with devastating accuracy, or if you can whip off a Rattler or two with good accuracy, your hitting the back of the jaw will be a really unpleasant experience for the guy. Remember the story I told you at the beginning of this book? It's the wad of nerves and glands that get slammed that makes getting pegged in the back of the jaw so unfun. So unless you're a gorilla who can palm Volkswagens or a 56th-degree black belt in who flung poo karate, forget straight shots to the jaw and come in from the side instead. You have a better chance of doing damage that way.

That's with the jaw shut—clamped, actually. You can *really* disjoint the jaw if you peg the guy while his mouth is open. This is where most "broken" jaws come from. Actually, they're sprained. Like the nose, they get displaced (and in this case, fractured). It's easier to break someone's jaw when he's got his mouth open. It's still no walk in the park, but it's easier. (Incidentally, did you know that you can get so ripped that when you pass out, if you do it at the wrong angle, your jaw will dislocate itself? It hangs down and slips out of joint. It can be popped back into place by someone wearing gloves who knows how to do it. In the meantime, though, you can't close your mouth. It's kind of funny if it's not happening to you.)

The Mouth

Here is a major bit of information that may shock the shit out of you. It has to do with the mouth. Do yourself a favor and don't bother hitting people in the mouth! The reason is two-fold. One, the mouth is backed up by bones. Bones are hard, and they hurt your hand (but we've gone through that before). Second—and this is the real motive behind avoiding the mouth as a target—is that this is one of the dirtiest, most bacteria-riddled portions of the body. Your body has a whole slew of defenses to make sure that the germs in your mouth don't get into it. (The tonsils, for instance. Taking out the tonsils is a really bad idea; they're the frontline of your immune system.) If you hit somebody in the mouth and cut your hand on his teeth, you can get seriously infected! I mean possibly hospital-time infected. No shit here, folks. There are people in jail on murder raps because they bit someone and the resulting wound festered and killed the schmuck. You wouldn't pee on an open wound, so don't have someone spit on one, either.

• • • • •

By now you've probably caught on that there are better places to hit than the face. The head in general is a rather poor target. If you're looking for a mind-fuck, have pinpoint accuracy, or if you have a fist that can smash through steel walls, the head and face can be targets. For the rest of us average grunts, it's time to look elsewhere.

CHAPTER FOUR

The Throat and Neck

Don't fight unless you're in the right.

—Oberon

Here are a couple of areas you should really think about before using them as targets. It's extremely easy to do permanent injury to somebody here. Yourself, for instance—third-degree murder is still something that they want to put you in prison for.

Both areas are extremely good targets, but for different reasons. For clarity, the neck is the sides and the back, while the throat is the front or tracheal area. In a sense, you can look at it like a figure eight: the smaller

smaller top circle is the throat, while the larger one on the bottom is the neck. There's a reason for this attention to detail, which will become obvious as we go along.

Your spine runs along the back of the neck. Aside from holding up your gourd, it also houses your spinal column. It's basically the trunk cable that runs your entire nervous system, which is why a broken neck is kind of a serious event. You can twist the wires in the neck enough that the whole system shuts down. That's one lethal variation. The other is arrived at via the throat.

There's this tube running down the middle of everything called the trachea. Not only is it important for speaking, it's sort of connected to this little process called breathing. This sucker is like a sectional hose. If you've ever bent a garden hose until it kinks and the water stops flowing, you'll understand why this is such a dangerous target. A hard enough punch to the throat will collapse someone's trachea and prevent air from getting to his lungs. In other words, he suffocates.

Now, in case you're going, "Oh boy, oh boy, oh boy, two goodie kill spots," put it on a leash. In case you haven't caught on yet, fighting is a dirty business, both during and after. If you were to take a little trip to your local penitentiary, you'd discover exactly how many people are in the pen because they lost their cool in a fight and did something extreme. Sure, they won the fight; they also killed somebody in front of twenty witnesses. Oops. This is the reality of the situation. Ask one of these guys if winning that fight was worth ten years of his life.

This is one of the reasons I stress the difference between fighting and combat. Face it, we all lose fights. I've lost a good share of mine and so has everyone else who has ever been around the block. It is the way of things. The fact that I am still breathing indicates that I have never lost in a combat situation. When I was a punk (and I admit I was), I got in a whole shitload of fights for no better reason than I had to show off how big my dick was. I was so scared that my dick didn't have a big red "S" tattooed on it, I went out and got myself into all sorts of shit just to prove what a he-man I was (mostly with people very much like myself). We all looked tough on the outside (at least to each other), but down deep we were scared that we weren't "MANLY." We all knew what it was about— John Wayne swaggering in and telling an entire barroom full of vicious characters, "That's the way it's gonna be, pilgrims." That's what being a man was, at least that's what we were told we had to do to be men.

In the meantime, we had to try and deny the fact that we were actually scared shitless. Although most of us hated the violence, it was all we had ever known. I hate to admit it, but we were raised with violence. At the movies, at school, and, for many of us, at home. The chaos of others' lives was the model presented to us as normal. We were given no choice; it seemed that violence was the only way, and that was that. If you weren't a victimizer, you were a victim. It seemed that the only way out of the whole mess was to be the absolute most badass motherfucker that ever came down the pikeway. That was the attraction: if we got good enough at it, we would be left alone by it. At least that's what we thought. There was something wrong with that theory, but we couldn't quite put our fingers on it. So we skittered around playing this game that wasn't a game, all of us trying to figure out what was wrong and why we were so scared.

Well, folks, there comes a point where all ugly scenes must come to an end. Here's the hitch: with violence, it's not a game. Sooner or later, you end up coming to the crossroads, and there, as at all crossroads, you can lose your soul to the devil. Combat is a crossroads. Once you've been there, it's never the same. How you get there, how fast you're going, what you do there, and what's inside of you will determine the outcome. Many people make the mistake of flying through this crossroads full-speed ahead. When the dust settles, they're in serious shit with no way out. Sometimes, something dies inside of them. Some part of them is frozen into a painful lump, and they basically turn into walking zombies.

Reality has to be faced, folks. People *die* in combat. It might be the other guy, or it might be you. It doesn't matter. Once you cross this line, there's no going back, and it will cost you something. The price depends on things inside you that most people don't like talking about. They try to deny that these things have anything to do with violence, which is like saying the mountain has nothing to do with mountain climbing.

In case you're wondering what the hell I'm talking about here, think about it this way: you can kill someone with a throat shot. Most people don't have any idea what that means. They think it's like the movies— somebody gets shot and falls down nice and clean. Bullshit. Even if you aren't the one who goes down, some part of you dies with each person who does. It hurts, 'cause it never really is buried with most people. It stays with them, a frozen ache that stinks of death, for everyone to smell. This is what people don't understand when they're playing tough. I really didn't understand it either until I had to remove from my carpet the blood of a partner that I loved like a brother. That's when it finally began to dawn on me that it wasn't a game. It was self-defense, and it had to be done, but that didn't make it any easier for the people involved. Actually, I lost two bro's that night, one to death and another to what happened afterward. That was the first and the worst. There have been other deaths and bloody battles since, and all of them have left scars. I've thawed much of the ice that once covered that part of my heart, but that smell of death is still strong in my nose. It doesn't really go away.

So remember, if you come speeding up to the crossroads without any breaks, you can easily take the way to Hell. One panic decision in a fight, one moment of uncontrolled temper, one blind moment of enraged, bruised ego, and you're in the shit for the rest of your life. (Or you blow it and the guy beats you to the draw, in which case you're dead and it doesn't much matter.)

It's not a movie out there. This is what it's really about—throwing up with the sick realization of what you've just done to a person. (And the sick realization that you've blown it in front of witnesses.) If there was no better reason than being in a pissed-off mood when it started, you might have just scorched your entire life in one monstrous ball of fire.

Yes, you can kill people using the information in this book. If you have to do somebody to protect a loved one or to save your life (not just win a fight), you're going to have to do it. That's what combat is actually about. You have no choice; the only way out is death or permanent injury for somebody.

It fucks you up. Plain and simple. (Of course, most of the people who get to this crossroads haven't really spent much time in introspection, and that's why they're there in the first place. It's easier to slug than it is to look inside. I know, 'cause I've done a lot of both. Eventually though, with that philosophy, you'll come to the crossroads. It's there that you have to decide what your course is.)

It's amazing what you'll see when you look at people who have been through this. Some have died inside and are waiting for their bodies to follow their souls. Others have condemned themselves to a living hell and let it destroy their lives. Some have turned to violence as a profession (of these people, some are twisted about it and others aren't).

Some keep on doing it. Without knowing why, they put themselves into these situations until one day they either wake up and walk away or blow it and are buried somewhere. Some people have totally suppressed what has happened and deny that aspect of themselves, trying to force their lives into safe little molds and definitions. Eventually, they either keel over with a heart attack or their carefully constructed world falls apart. A few people accept it as only a part of them and proceed to live successful lives (maybe not monetarily, but in the sense that they can look themselves in the mirror in the morning and accept and forgive).

The last place is where you have to end up somehow. (In case you're wondering, I was the kind that kept on doing it until one day I woke up and said, "Like it or not, I've got to deal with it." I did, and you know what? It was the hardest, most terrifying thing I have ever done in my life; at the same time, it was the greatest and most freeing action I have ever taken. Once I figured it out I went batshit for about a year. It's that bad.)

Now, a lot of people arrive at this crossroads with the he-man act, but once there they back down. What's bad about this is it sticks in their craw. They've never forgiven themselves for not crossing that line. Somewhere down deep is a gnawing pain, because they think they're not real men. In one sense, they've never grown up. Raised with violence, they know only violence; yet, they don't think they're men. This shame erupts often in the form of violence, but they never risk it with someone who can fight back. Instead, they take it home and beat on their wives or kids. Some become masters of cheap shots and ambushes, attacking people from behind. Others become rapists. The variety is endless, but the end result is the same. They take it out on those who are weaker than themselves and can't fight back.

What's really bad about this, and what drove me up the wall for a time, is that these people are the ones that really keep the fucked-up myth of supermen going. It's not the guys who've crossed the line who are trying to prove something to themselves or others. Kids who are around this sort of pseudo-superman are raised trying to be what this guy is ashamed about not being. These fuckers cause a lot more damage to the human race than the emotionally dead killers who only drop people who cross them.

The reason I've just screamed off into left field for such a long time is to let you people know that there is more on the line here than just punching somebody. Who you are is worth more than your injured pride. Blowing your entire life in one flash of anger over some piddly-shit comment is not worth it. I wish somebody had told me when I was younger that it was okay to lose a fight now and then. Maybe then I wouldn't have pushed it to the level I thought was necessary.

In my life, I have seriously hurt people with violence. The fact that it was done to me does not make my actions right. There have been times where violence was the proper course of action, and I do not regret those times. The damage I did was in the name of defense—that of myself or others. I admit, though, that there were times when violence was not the proper course. Whether I was doing it for ego, anger, pride, money, or some other reason does not mean I was right. I was both lucky and good, which is why, unlike so many of the people I used to run with, I am not dead, in prison, or burned out.

If you're interested in living a long and fruitful life, you had better think about what I've been talking about here. *Throat and neck shots can and will kill if done correctly.* They are not to be used lightly to avoid losing a fight. If you have friends with you, they should drag you away from a fight before it gets too ugly, and you should do the same for them. Either way, the idea is to keep everyone alive and/or out of prison if at all possible.

The Throat

That said, let's look at the throat as a target. Running along both sides of the trachea is what is commonly referred to as the "jugular." While the throat is potentially a deadly target, it can also be extremely good for conveying how seriously annoyed you are about being bothered.

A fast, *LIGHT* Setup to the throat will cause the trachea to flatten, cutting off the airflow for a split second. This is a major shock to the system, and the effects can range from mild shock and momentary paralysis to total body collapse in a coughing/choking/vomiting fit.

This is one of those moves I prefer to use when facing several potential opponents. Drop one hard with a throat punch and the others may reconsider tangling with you (especially if you step back and tell them to get their buddy to a hospital, reminding them that moments wasted fighting you may result in their friend's death). The other option is to drop one of them this way and immediately go after another with an attack that's just as friendly. On the other hand, you can drop one of them and run through the hole you've just created, which is my all-time favorite. No sense in messing around when you're outnumbered. Pop and run—it's more likely to save your ass.

A throat shot makes a definite statement about the caliber of person you are. This can swing one of two ways: either the guy(s) will back off right there and then, or you are going into the shit right now. Since the throat shot can be a killing move, somebody *might* decide to take umbrage at the fact that you've just done something that could have killed them. (It's a strange quirk of human nature, but that's the way it is.)

In case you haven't figured it out yet, when you're in a fight you should keep your chin down to protect your throat. It prevents the odd punch that glances off your chin and into your throat. This added bit of protection will keep you smiling much longer.

Up to this point I've been talking about flattening somebody's trachea, which is fine and dandy, but it's not the only way to torque somebody's wa by way of the throat. Most people do a lousy job of trying to strangle somebody, probably because they haven't really decided if they are trying to cut off the windpipe or tear it out. I once tried to strangle a guy, and I spent some time trying to figure out what had gone wrong. Once again, it fell back to what I had seen on TV being bullshit. (You see, as much of a pain in the ass as actors can be, most directors don't really want to kill them off. This is because there is a thing called "dailies," which you usually get either late at night or the day after filming. The directors watch these to see how the shoot turned out. If something went wrong, they're going to have to reshoot the scene. If you were actually to kill the actors, you couldn't reshoot it. See? It makes sense after all.)

In a cinema strangle, the guy wraps his hands around somebody's throat and squeezes (usually a young, pretty, half-naked extra who's playing the part of a bimbo too stupid to run from a wacko wandering around wearing a hockey mask). The fingers are supposedly digging into the back of the neck while the thorax is crushed by the power that countless repeats have given the psycho-killer's thumbs . . . *wrong*. This is what I tried to do, and I found myself wondering why the guy still had enough energy to keep on slugging me until people pulled me off of him.

Well, first off, grab your thumb and bend it back. The fact that you can do that indicates that the actual thumb is not where your power to cut off somebody's windpipe is going to come from. Now, grab yourself the way you've seen it done in the movies and dig your fingers in. In case you didn't notice, you're probably poking neck muscle. Fat lot of good that's going to do. It's *muscle*, people; muscle takes abuse better than anything else we've got. So while this strangling technique looks good and hurts like hell, it's basically ineffective.

Okay, let go of yourself before you turn purple and look at your hand again. See the "V" where your thumb connects with your hand? Ah ha! If you apply straight pressure from that point, the amount of force absorbed by the thumb is limited. This means the pressure goes where you want it to. Now, if you curl your fingers in and begin to dig in, they should be on the jugular rather than in muscle. Pinching here creates the necessary blockage of both air and blood to do the job.

That's the slow way to get your point across. Any maiming-style attack to the throat is a real attention-getter. Remember at the beginning of the chapter when I mentioned the figure eight shape of this area? The throat is extremely vulnerable to maiming techniques. You can grab the small part of the eight and try to pinch it out, but it is possible to rip somebody's throat out this way, so you'd better be serious about playing crab.

Now, this doesn't have to be fatal. In fact, if you slam somebody up against the wall and squeeze this way, you'll get your point across. I know a biker and former bouncer named Chuck who just loves this move. The wall helps, as will any large piece of furniture, because it prevents the guy from trying to jerk out of the grip. (Like, where's he going to go? Chuck also has hands that could swat a water buffalo senseless.) Since I have little paws I like to use obstacles.

I should point out that this move is extremely effective against young fighting bucks with big dicks and little brains. You know the sort—the ones who for some stupid-ass reason get in your face with their chests puffed out, arms thrown back, and nuts totally exposed. I guess they think they're showing that they're so tough that they don't have to protect themselves. My biggest problem with that type is deciding which tempting target I want to rip off and hand to them.

Anyway, if you use this move it does help to have strong hands. Also, be aware that if the guy is real long on testosterone and real short on brains, he'll probably try to swing on you. So be ready to take a punch or two until the guy realizes that the more he hits, the less air he's going to get for breathing. It takes about two hits, maximum, before this sinks in. Your snarling "stop that or I'll kill you" might get the message across a little faster, though.

It's annoying but true—every now and then you'll get somebody who will panic when you try to strangle him. (I personally think this is rather bohemian of them, but not everyone has the class and savoir-faire I do.) So expect a reaction along these lines: the guy may decide to slip a knife into you, kick you in the nuts, claw your eyes out, or some other unpleasant thing. What you might want to do about this depends on how you grabbed him.

If you grabbed him with your left hand (so you could punch with your stronger right) and he pulls a weapon, you either need to let go or rip his throat out right there. If he's just trying to hurt you with his hands, rattle his teeth a few times and tell him to hold still. If, however, you're holding him with your right hand, your left is available to block any attacks he might consider initiating. If he goes for a weapon in his pocket, you can proceed to squeeze and pin his hand. *Do not ever let the guy's hands out of your sight when you are doing this!* If you do, it is seriously likely that you are going to get hurt.

Now, getting out of a stranglehold is amazingly simple. In fact, once you know how to get out of one you'll probably never want to use this type of attack again. Aside from what I just told you about the guy whaling on you while you're trying to choke him, the move has some serious limitations.

The first way to break a stranglehold is the standard: snake your arms up in between his and then spread them. Theoretically, this should break his grip. If, however, the guy is bigger or stronger (the two not necessarily being synonymous), this isn't going to work well. I would advise snaking in an eye shot before trying this one anyway—if the guy is stronger, it's mandatory.

The second way is a trick I picked up from Peyton Quinn, who has put out an excellent couple of videos on self-defense. (The man covers the basics of fighting like nobody I've seen. His style is plain, simple, and across-the-board. I highly recommend *Self-Defense against the Sucker Puncher* and *Defending against the Blade*, which are also available from Paladin Press.)

His version is to grab one of the guy's hands and lock it down. Yep, your left hand is grabbing his right, and you're holding him to you. I know it sounds like the absolute wrong thing to do, but trust me for a second here. Next, you snake your right hand up between his forearms. Again, I recommend an eyeshot before going on any further, but that's just me. Anyway, whether you poke his eyes or not, continue to snake your arm up between his, past your elbow and toward your upper arm. Now, begin to twist to your left and stick his pinned forearm into your armpit. By shoving your shoulder between his arms, you'll break his grip on your throat. The neat thing is, you're in a primo place to throw an elbow strike to his jaw or throat, followed by a hip throw. Neat, huh?

The Neck

Let's look at the neck. There are books out on how to snap somebody's neck. One of the problems I've noticed in these is that the unfortunate snappee is usually tied to a chair. If you can get the guy to volunteer to be tied up so you can snap his neck, more power to you. I wouldn't bet on it, though.

This is another one of those "it's possible, but" situations. If you could sneak up and surprise someone, you might be able to snap his neck, but your straddling in a wide stance behind him is probably going to tip him off that something is amiss. Furthermore, you're probably going to encounter some resistance to your endeavors. More than likely, this will result in some seriously sprained vertebrae disks and muscles.

If, however, you have the muscle to do this sort of thing, you really don't need to know the technique. Any flaws in style will be more than made up for by muscle. For those of you who don't have to wear platform shoes to keep your knuckles from dragging, it's time to look at the more practical side of the neck as a target.

Before you think about going for the neck as a target, take a look at the guy you're facing. Does he look like Ichabod Crane, with a scrawny neck that an oversized head sort of teeters around on? Or does he, like a guy I know named Big John, have a head that slopes into shoulders, with no real visible neck? If the latter is the case, I'd advise looking at the kneecaps as alternative targets.

An impact to the side of the neck is another one of those ball-shot equivalents that are such a drag to deal with. Part of the reason it hurts so much to take one to the family jewels is that the pelvis is jammed into the spinal cord. This, in part, is why the nausea sweeps up and the rubber suddenly infests the legs. The trunk cable just got jammed, big time. The operator comes on to tell you your call cannot be completed as dialed.

The same thing happens when you get knocked alongside the neck. A Leopard Punch to the side of the neck can get a tilt sign out of somebody incredibly fast. Why not—it just jammed the circuits in a seriously unpleasant way. Try taking a swing at yourself and you'll see what I mean. Unlike the balls, it doesn't hurt with just a graze. (You know, the ones where your balls do the paddleball imitation—stretch to the end of the string and then come slamming back, twap!) A good solid hit here should take the wind out of most people's sails.

For some reason, it hurts less to be hit on the back of the neck. It takes less pressure to dislocate the neck from this angle, though, because there is less muscle there to protect it. I don't know why we're designed this way, but it's true.

Let's talk about dislocating or breaking for a

moment. One thing that scares me is how vulnerable the neck is to attack. If you manage to dislocate or somehow break somebody's neck by force and he doesn't die, there is a very good chance that he will be paralyzed for life. This is why I prefer not to strike the back of the neck. The risk is less if you go for the side because of all the muscles there. Death and paralysis are still possibilities, however, so be careful.

Undoubtedly, the throat is the easiest, most accessible, potentially lethal target that the Average Joe can opt for. The bad side of this is that it *could* happen to you or your friends during a scuffle, either intentionally or accidently. (There is a procedure called an emergency tracheotomy that you should know how to do. It involves a pen tube and cutting a hole in the trachea to keep someone from suffocating. I'm not a medic, so I'm not going to tell you how to do it. But I do know how to do it, and I strongly advise you to learn it as well, especially if you're going to put this target sector in your bag of tricks. That way, if you crush his windpipe, you're not up on a murder rap.)

One of the things I've learned, along with tearing people apart, is how to put them back together. If you're going to be sparring a lot, I suggest you pick up some basic massage techniques. Knowing how the human body is put together is part of fighting; knowing how to put yourself and your friends back together after a fight is part of surviving. For somebody who has gone through as much shit as I have, I am in incredible shape. Most people I know who have gone through the sort of things that I have are in much worse shape. There are two reasons I'm in as good of shape as I am: one, I knew how to put myself back together again; and two, I wasn't so stupidly macho that I couldn't backpedal. *Learn how to heal as well as hurt.* It'll save you all sorts of shit starting ten years down the line and lasting the rest of your life. (Besides, you learn massage, and you'll be amazed how popular you become with the ladies . . . heh, heh, heh.)

Anyway, throat and neck shots are extremely effective, but you do have to be careful when, where, and how you use them.

CHAPTER FIVE

The Body

Don't hit the guy in the face where it shows, hit him in the body.
That way, he can claim you beat him up, but he can't prove it
because nothing shows.

—Art Payne

The body is where most fights can be resolved without too much permanent damage. Amazingly enough, it's also misused or totally ignored by many people as a target. That's because they think there's nothing there but bone and muscle. This is sort of true about the chest, but totally wrong about the lower portion.

I think the real reason people skip over the body as a target is that most don't know how to throw an uppercut. It's weird, but in all the fights I've seen, I'd have to say the uppercut is probably one of the most ignored moves. I personally like them and use them a lot. Maybe it's the way most people think about anger and fighting that keeps their blows aimed up high. We'll go into that more in a moment, but right now I want to stress something very important.

Most people in Western society cut themselves and others off at the neck. They seem to think the person is in the head, and the body is just something that comes along as a vehicle. That's why when most people throw a punch, it's to the head—they think they're hitting the whole person. This is a serious mistake. A person is a whole body, not just a head riding around on a machine. *When you fight somebody, your target area is the entire body, not just the head and shoulders!*

Like it or not, it's true, so shift your attention away from individual parts and begin to look at the whole person. Once you get the hang of it you'll see that most people don't pay attention to the lower parts of their bodies. This is the biggest mistake you can make against a streetfighter, 'cause he'll use it against you if you leave it flapping out in the wind.

First off, most people are poorly developed below their necks. Some people have big chests and arms but dwindle down from there. Others are sort of pear-shaped and soft. Others look like walking sticks. Most body types are a rather sorry state of affairs.

Some, though, are like walking tanks—big tubes of muscle that sort of descend straight to the ground. And there are those who are thin but are actually like piano wire wrapped around a skeleton, the proverbial lean and mean. There are also people who are built like bears and lumber through anything in their way. Still others are like wolverines, little bundles of muscles and fangs.

Before you even think about throwing a punch, look at what you're up against. This is important because you fight a big guy differently than a small guy. The same thing is true about fighting a skinny guy or a fat guy. The body type of the guy you're jamming with will affect how he fights.

I'm not a big guy. In my boot heels I come to about 5'9". This supposedly makes me a weaker and smaller opponent—until you get me into a closed area that you can't move around in. Then you discover it's not a matter of you catching me; I've caught you. You've crawled into a badger's den and are suddenly in it tight. This is a range of fighting called "infighting."

Infighting is preferred by shorter people and those with shorter arms. It's a fast, sharp, and curved form of fighting in a smaller arena. This is one area where you're at a serious disadvantage if you have longer arms. There are two reasons for this: one, the guy's all over you, and two, you're in an area of limited mobility.

A friend I used to spar with, on the other hand, is 6'1" and basically a pair of legs attached to a platform that carries his head. Taekwon-do was his preferred form, and in an open space, the guy was pure hell to contend with. Those long legs would kick you into tomorrow if you didn't get out of the way or rush him.

He was what is called a "distance fighter." He wanted you to stay about two to four feet away from him so he could damage you. From that range, he made sure you'd end up collecting your teeth from the ground.

Needless to say, when he and I would spar, we'd each try to keep the other in our stronger range. I'd either have to charge him or retreat into areas where his size was a disadvantage. He'd try to keep me away and not get cornered in a cramped area. Since our impromptu sparring matches could happen at any time and in any place, it was really interesting.

When you're about to get into it with someone, look at his body. Is he likely to be a distance fighter? An infighter? Are you in an area where you can use his range against him? An infighter is at a serious disadvantage in a empty parking lot, while a distance fighter is not exactly in the hottest position in a crowded bar.

Know your opponent's weak spots. If the guy has a chest and set of arms that should belong to a gorilla instead of a human, look lower. Are his midsection and legs well developed? If not, you've got your targets. Is he the same size or taller than you are? If he's taller, then uppercuts will work well, while straight shots to the chest and face are a waste of time. If the guy is shorter than you are, you could be in trouble. You'll be hitting down on a well-armored portion. That means it's time to kick low. A tank of a person is not going to be as fast as a wiry little dude, but he will be better armored by muscle. You'll have to fight them differently. (By the way, don't rely on big guys being slow. I've met up with some motherin' fast big guys.)

Back to uppercuts. As I said, one of the things that never ceases to amaze me is that people don't use this lovely punch nearly enough. When done right, it carries the bulk of the body's weight. It's fast and flexible. What's more, it's a real bitch to block.

Blocking an uppercut is more of a friction-and-deflection process than anything else. Due to the circular nature of the blow, a straight block doesn't really work against it. You must both deflect the blow and slow it down with pressure. Otherwise, it's going to slide in anyway. Be aware that it takes practice to understand what the hell I'm talking about.

On to target areas, most of which actually concern the angle of strike and such. Let's look at the first one and you'll see what I mean.

The Shoulders

The shoulder muscles are good targets for cumulative damage. A strike to the trapezius muscle will cause pain and slow muscle reaction. That doesn't mean it will stop him, it'll just slow him down and make it hurt when he moves.

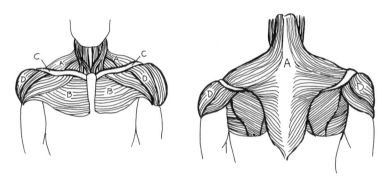

The shoulders: A—trapezius, B—pectoralis major, C—collar bone, D—deltoid.

A straight punch to the shoulders is sort of like trying to hit a fly with a .357. It can be done, but you'll more than likely miss. Any of the downward swatting strikes (Bear, Dragon, Hanging, or even Knife Hand) are really effective here. The muscles do have nerve centers underneath, so impact here can cause momentary paralysis. If you've ever been given a "Pony Bite" (where somebody grabs you by the trap muscle and squeezes, not unlike the Vulcan Nerve Pinch), you'll know how much it hurts. It doesn't actually do too much damage, but it's real uncomfortable.

About three inches lower and to the front is another story altogether. Here lies one of the greatest weaknesses in the entire chest area, the collarbone. You've got two, one on either side. Any well-placed downward strike technique can break these puppies. The target area is actually the middle of the bone (closer to the throat than the shoulder). Either end of the bone is supported by more bone structure. Cracking someone's collar bone usually takes the fight out of them rather effectively.

The Chest and Back

The chest is one of those targets that is basically immune to any broad-striking-surface blow. Face it, it's a massive shock absorber made of muscle and bone. The very nature of the chest is to move out and in by muscle contraction. To do any damage, you have to expend a massive amount of energy to move it further than it's supposed to go. It's easier to break something that's fixed than something that's flexible. The chest is a damn good example of a flexible-but-solid system.

Now that we know flat punches against the chest are basically a waste of time, what do we use instead? Those of you who said "reduced-striking-surface punches" can stay after class and clean the chalkboard erasers. Now add focused targeting to the reduced striking surfaces.

Yes, indeed, folks! Those old reduced-striking-surface blows just love to mosey on down to that there spread of chest area. Why, I tell you, jes' a quick little Phoenix Punch to the pectoral muscles will put a cramp in anybody's style. 'Specially if'n y'all come in from the side and sorta slide it in just under the muscle. I tell ya, it'll let that there goat roper know right where it sits. (Thank you for that lovely bit of information there, Tex. As soon as we get a translator in, we'll figure out exactly what in hell you just said.) In the meantime, let's look at why reduced striking surfaces work on this area.

It all has to do with muscles. Unlike other areas of the body, where you're trying to do deep damage, the chest is an area where you should go for surface muscle damage. That's because everything is connected to the chest and back muscles. Do a little experiment. Stick your finger into your chest muscle, push in hard, and move your arm around. Comes a point when you begin to feel it pull around your poking finger, right?

Yes indeed, folks, it's all connected. Hurt the chest muscles and you slow down your opponent's arms. This means both his blocks and punches are slower. Ta da! Speed may not be everything, but it does make up a sizable chunk of this business.

Now, I want to show you something. Look at the illustration below. You will notice that the two major muscle-group areas on the torso are in the front and in the back. Better known as the pectorals (pecs) and latissimus dorsi (lats). These muscle groups are, in short, real fuckin' strong. In fact, they act as a form of soft armor.

Targeting in this area means striking at areas that

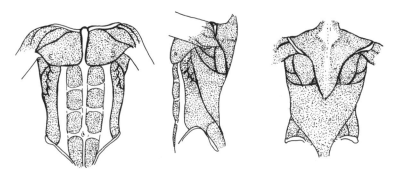

Front, back, and side views of the human trunk.

are not armored too well (like the sides) or coming in beneath the armor. Now, mind you, we're only talking about muscles here; we'll get to bones in a bit. The area where the major muscle groups connect to the rib cage is a primo target. Here's a little experiment. First, flex your chest muscles, then poke yourself in the middle of one of your pecs with one finger. Do it hard, maybe a few times.

Okay, sure, you felt it, but it didn't hurt all that much. In fact, there's a possibility that your finger folded up from the impact. Like I said, armor. The next stage is to reach around and find where your pecs connect to your chest right in front of your armpit. Do the same poking routine.

Hurts doesn't it? Basically, what you are doing is coming in underneath the armor and straining the connecting tendons that hold the muscles in place. Watch how boxers cover this part of their bodies during matches. From this angle, damage tolls can accumulate real God damn quick.

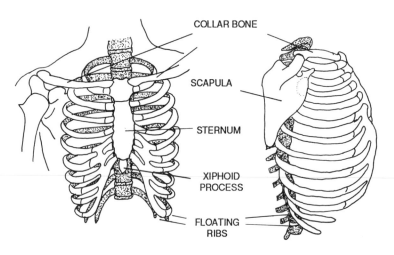

The rib cage, front and side view.

The same can be said of the muscles in the back. Your lats are an incredibly easy target for someone throwing a hook when you're face-to-face, or someone throwing a straight punch if you're in some of the Oriental-type stances. Getting hit here really hurts like a mother. So, a reduced-surface strike straight into the muscle is damaging, but not as much as a reduced-surface strike under the muscles. Unless you're Godzilla, a flat punch straight to the chest is about as useless as pissing on a forest fire.

Let's deepen our perspective here and move on to the bones of the chest. Take a look at the illustration on page 100.

See that thing on the front of the chest that looks like a spider with horns? It's called the sternum. The sternum is made out of bone, as are the ribs. You'll notice, though, that there's stuff that connects the ribs to the sternum. Guess what? It's not bone; it's cartilage. (Yeah, the same flexible stuff that makes up your ears and nose.) See, if your rib cage was made entirely of bone, you couldn't move your chest, which means that you couldn't breathe. You'll notice that there's more cartilage on the bottom than on the top. This compresses and moves. (Remember this, there will be a test later.)

Although it takes some hellacious force to bust the sternum, here's a trick that an old streetfighter taught me. It's handy at preventing trouble when you apply it right. You take your finger, lock it down really good and tight, and poke the guy who's giving you trouble in the sternum. Do it right and it hurts like hell. To the average guy who doesn't know about reduced striking surfaces, it hurts way out of proportion to what's being used. More than likely, he'll be asking himself, if you can do that with just a finger, what could you do if you decided to use your whole hand?

Again, this isn't something you can do just off the

bat. It takes practice. Also, there are a couple of ways to cheat by the way that you hold your hand. And if you time this move right, you can use the impacts to punctuate what you're saying, which can realign the guy's reality.

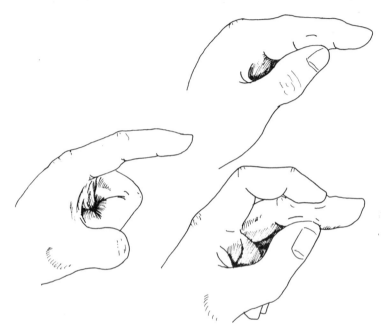

Sternum-thumping hand positions.

You'll notice that in two of the three hand positions, the thumb braces the second finger bone, acting as both shock absorber and strut. In none of the options is the finger held straight. Fingers are most often dislocated at the second joint; going in with the finger held straight is just asking to get it dislocated.

Notice anything about the way the ribs at the top differ from the ribs at the bottom? (That large hunk of bone on the top, called the sternum, is a major clue.)

While they all slant down, the ones at the bottom slant down more. This is because they aren't connected to the sternum as the top ones are, but they cover the lungs. All of this structural design affects how different parts of the rib cage can take impact.

The ones at the top, which have less of a downward slant, are independently connected to the sternum and spine. In one sense, they form a very secure bridge to protect the top of the lungs. Any impact here is going to be transmitted throughout the entire framework and the energy will be diffused to the point of harmlessness. (So you know that this sort of thing works, bulletproof vests work on the same principle of diffusion of energy.)

Let's take a gander at the lower ribs. What's this we see? They are not connected to anything other than each other and are at more of a downward slant. The slant means that they are less able to take an impact without compressing. It's sort of like taking an inner tube and standing it up. If you hit it in a downward motion, it will take the impact and flex because of its shape. No real damage. It stays standing upright. If, however, you strike it at a forty-five-degree angle from the top, it will fall over. Its structure isn't designed to support it against that sort of blow. Same thing with your ribs. Hitting the upper ones is like hitting the inner tube straight on, while hitting the lower ones is like hitting it at an angle—you'll get better results.

The last two ribs—the floating ribs—aren't connected at all. They're only vulnerable to a hook to the side or a shot to the lower back, but getting nailed here is a seriously unpleasant event. Aside from squeezing your lungs, a blow to this area flattens your kidneys. I had to drop out of a rough-'n-tumble once because I took a spinning heel kick here. I sort of hobbled over and sat the rest of that one out.

The fact that they aren't well connected and are

actually more of a protective flap than a structural support makes the lower ribs an A#1 target. When you hit someone here it compresses the ribs into the lungs and diaphragm. This causes physical pain and affects the breathing process of your opponent. Since most people don't breathe correctly anyway, especially during a fight, this can screw them up big time.

Let's stop something here for a second. In the Western world, we are taught to go head-to-head with trouble. Well, that's what we are told we're supposed to do. In actuality, backbiting, setups, ambushes, cheap shots, con jobs, and passive-aggressive behavior are more the norm than head-to-head confrontations. Nobody talks about how the game is *really* played, especially not to you younger folks out there. Well, not only are they not practicin' what they're preachin', they're setting you up to get nailed by not telling you the truth. In my opinion, one of the best ways to lie is to tell only half the truth. Think about it that way and you begin to wonder just what people are leaving out when they tell you something.

The "whys" and "how come they do that" ain't my concern here. Those are monsters you're going to have to wrestle on your own. What I am concerned with is letting you people know how the game is really played so you don't get creamed out there by something that you ain't never heard of. Part of this is to get you to thinking in different ways than you've been taught. The difference is that I'm not telling you how to think, I'm telling you to start noticing things that you were told not to notice before. The way you think is up to you. All I can say is that the stuff I'm pointing out to you is not only important, it might just save your life one day.

Something that is really underplayed in what we are taught is how important our support system is.

The truth is, without it, we're effectively fucked. It doesn't matter who or what the situation is, this is true. The support system is critical for survival. What's more, our support system is vulnerable unless we take care to protect it. Again, we usually don't think about this, but it's of major importance. I don't care how big or strong the guy is, he needs air to breath. Look at the German army during World War II. Rommel had the Allies' asses kicked. (Patton was the only guy who could handle him, but command wouldn't let him come out and play.) So here's Rommel zipping around Africa in better tanks than the Allies, with better strategies, generally raising hell, and with nobody to stop him. What happens? He runs out of gas! The German supply lines went down! The same thing with the Battle of the Bulge. They ran out of gas! Their supply lines went kaput! All of their superior this, that, and the other thing were useless because of a weak supply line. That's because the Allies were bombing the shit out of their factories and refineries. The reason that Germany lost the Second World War is because of supplies! *Their support system failed!* The same thing happens to people! Savvy?

What all of this leads up to is how we are taught to think in the Western world: the way to win is to be stronger than your opponent. Actually, that's horseshit. The way to win is to be less vulnerable than your opponent. There is a subtle but important difference there. The greatest warriors are those whose shields are equally distributed—they are balanced in their self-protection. They don't leave something exposed to doubly protect something else. You need to start thinking of ways to ensure your support systems. Sometimes this means armor; other times it means other things. Mostly, though, it means that you need to know what human weak points are in general, and what your weak points are specifically, and cover them both.

Most people are like the ancient Celts when it comes to protection. These guys used to think that only sissies wore armor. It was a manly thing to go into battle without armor. In fact, they'd go into battle buck-naked to prove they weren't wearing any. They were into really big shields, though. They'd run into battle bare-assed naked, lugging this huge shield with them. They thought this was macho and a stand-up fight, a guaranteed good time for all. The Romans kicked their asses.

Face it, having one big shield while your dick hangs out in the wind is not a good way to win a fight. Most people are like the Celts when it comes to this sort of insanity. They think they have to do a stand-up macho thing and stomp their opponent. They put all their energy into one big honking shield, while leaving all sorts of important shit flapping free. Unfortunately, when they realize that they've left their asses uncov-ered, they're usually in the process of getting torn off.

Let's look at another group, the "retarded" cousins of the Celts, called the Picts. These guys weren't big and blond (or redheaded) like the Celts. In fact, they were sort of short and dark. The big, beautiful Celts thought these little guys were savages and shooed them off into what's now Scotland. There were enough of them to hold Scotland, but not enough to kick the Celts out of the rest of England and Ireland. So they settled down. They hung around and threw rocks at each other, howled at the moon, and generally had a good time being Robert E. Howard prototypes.

Then along came the Romans. (Gasp!) The Picts' macho Celtic cousins had gotten the shit kicked out of them in toe-to-toes with the Romans. Well, the Romans marched farther north and got a rude fuckin' surprise. The Picts didn't wear armor either, but it didn't matter, 'cause you never saw the little shits. The quickest way to tell that a Pict was around was from the arrow stickin' out of your buddy. You'd wake up in the middle of the night to find your tent on fire, thirty guys with their throats slit, and your supplies gone. It wasn't Avon calling. When they did fight, they'd pop out of nowhere, poke some people, and then disappear in grass that you'd swear a gopher couldn't hide in. The classic military term for this is "a fuckin' ambush!" Finally, the Romans built a couple of walls to keep these little shits out. The Picts were happy—they went back to throwing rocks at each other and barking at the moon. Meanwhile, Rome came and went.

These guys didn't care that they didn't have armor. The only time you need armor is in a stand-up fight, and they weren't into stand-up fights. What they could do, though, is not only live off, but with, the land. They were perfectly able to get along with what they had. You couldn't cut their supply lines, because there weren't any to cut. They'd only fight when they wanted to and on their own terms. In case you haven't noticed, anytime someone tangles with folks under these conditions, it's bad news. Actually, America got its start by doing exactly that against the British, and you'd think we'd have caught on to the effectiveness of this style by messing with the Apaches and the Vietcong.

Now what all of this muttering leads up to is the fact that you have to look at yourself. How much support do you need, both as a human being and as an individual? What I'm talking about is directly related to fighting, and it can go as deep as you want it to. You need to realize, though, that you need certain things in a confrontation. One of them is air. Plain and simple— no air, no fight. That's why a punch to the throat can end a fight real quick. No breathey, no fighty. It takes away your support system.

The same applies with other things. Balance, for instance—if he ain't standing, he ain't fighting, so trip him. Also, he ain't so tough alone, so if you're going to fight him, catch him alone. Along the same lines, beer in the eyes stings like shit. If he's blinded, he ain't fighting. All sorts of important details can determine whether the guy is going to fight or not. Most people consider taking advantage of these kinds of things as cheap shots, back bites, ambushes, and related annoyances. They cling to the belief that these sorts of things are chickenshit and not how it's actually done. Sorry folks, it is the way it works. Hanging on to the bullshit lies of how it's "supposed to be" will get you nailed to the wall by someone who operates this way. Most people (in life in general, and fighting in particular) go down because they don't know how to look at things this way. Because of this blindness, they can't see that they are actually being threatened in their most vulnerable spot until it's too late. Your supply lines are as important as what's happening on the frontline. One without the other is dogmeat.

Start looking for something you can take away from the guy that will aid your cause. Like the ancient Celts, most people leave crucial support lines totally unprotected, because we are told not to pay attention to these sorts of things. That's poor training you can use to your advantage: while your opponents aren't paying any attention to their weak spots, you're covering yours.

That's why lower-rib shots are so damned effective. Three or four Rattlers to the lower rib cage and the guy's breathing is shot to shit. These hurt like hell, both when they hit and when the guy takes a breath.

It will slow him down like an anchor. Watch boxers in the ring. They are always guarding their lower ribs with their elbows. These guys are professional fighters who know how to minimize the damage they're going to take. The fact that they cover their short ribs ought to tell you something about the importance of this area as a target.

When you're in a fight, keep your sides protected. This is what I was talking about when I said that most people don't think below the neck during a fight. Just from the damage standpoint, you have to think of your entire body as a potential target. And remember that your supply lines are equally vulnerable to attack. Spend time and energy protecting everything of yours, while looking for the chance to foul up the other guy's lines. Lastly, if you have no protection for an area, don't leave it hanging out there in a toe-to-toe. Fall back and try again when the time is better for you than for your opponent.

While we're on the subject of supply lines, let's look at the area just below the sternum that's between, but not covered by, the lower ribs: the diaphragm.

Officially, the diaphragm is like a sheet of skin and muscle that separates your chest cavity from your abdominal region. In other words, it separates your lungs from your guts. The diaphragm also helps you breathe. Are the little bells going off yet? You got it, booby. If it's important to breathing, it's important as a target!

Any uppercut into this area is effective. How hard you hit determines how much it affects the guy. How you hold your hand also counts for a shitload. Reduced-surface blows are a real mother in this area. Since there are no bones here to absorb the blow, anything you give *gets*. If you've ever had the wind knocked out of you, you know what this one is about. Odds are that someone clobbered you here on purpose, with the express intent of knocking the wind out of you.

When we get the wind knocked out of us, a couple of things are actually happening at once. It seems that we have pockets of air in our lungs that aren't exhaled. They hang out and wait for you to exhale. When that happens, they go to work supplying oxygen to you while you're getting ready to inhale again. This is why when you're breath is out, you don't feel like you're suffocating. When you get nailed in the diaphragm, it forces these little pockets of air out. Sort of like sitting on a whoopie cushion. The other thing that happens is that the diaphragm goes into spasms when you hit it. That means it locks up for a bit before returning to its natural process.

The diaphragm is especially a prime target if you're smaller than the guy you're fighting. The shorter guy has the advantage in getting to this target area. He's striking up, while the bigger guy has to throw a seriously weird uppercut. If you're fighting a smaller guy, you really have to protect this part of your anatomy. Shedding and spinning are good things to remember at such a time. It's better to take a graze along the short ribs than it is to get one in the diaphragm.

Along the same lines is the xiphoid process, a piece of bone at the bottom of the sternum that can be snapped off easily by heavy impact. If the xiphoid process should pierce the diaphragm, it will cause it to go into spasms and possibly lead to suffocation. Talk about cutting off somebody's supply lines. . . .

On to the soft underbelly. Truth is (at least the truth according to anthropologists and chiropractors), we aren't quite done evolving yet. According to some high-falutin' muck-a-mucks, we are in the transitional phase between hopping around on all fours and having the perfected design for walking around on only two legs.

Most of this has to do with spinal structure and other related things that go wrong with us. But let us take a look at it from another standpoint, that of our stomachs.

Unlike our four-footed cousins whose backs protect theirs, our bellies are woefully unprotected. Oops. Against claws, fangs, and talons, we're in deep trouble. Against punches and kicks, it's not as bad, but it still ain't no picnic. All those funny bags, tubes, and sponges in there aren't really designed to take too much of an impact. They sort of squish in uncomfortable and funny-looking ways when pressed.

When I was a young, cockstrong punk, my buddies and I would play a game where we would tighten our stomach muscles and have somebody else punch us. (We also had another stupid game called "suicide," where four or five guys would go into a handball court and throw the ball against the wall. The rules were easy—if you dropped the ball or if it hit you, it was open season on you until you could touch the front wall. Nowhere did I say we were very bright.) The idea of the punch game was to see how hard we could punch someone in the stomach before his muscles gave out. Since we had time to tighten our not-yet-beer-softened stomach muscles, no real damage was done.

The effectiveness of the stomach as a target depends on who you're up against. If the guy has gone soft around the middle from too many beers under his belt, it's a good target. If the guy has got a set of stomach muscles that you could wash clothes on, it's probably not going to do any damage unless you seriously plug him. The good news is that flat, washboard stomachs are sort of rare in people over twenty-one.

Another good piece of information is that a lot of people (myself included) hate sit-ups. This means that there's a whole slew of people running around with seriously strong arms, chests, and back muscles, who are weak in the stomach. Hell, when I'm not moving the computer keys, I move furniture, and my stomach is going soft on me. (Not for long after putting this in black and white. I ain't no fool.) Since there's a thunderin' herd of people who suffer the same weakness, it's something you have to protect on yourself and target on others.

A hard shot to the abdomen hurts like a mother. Uppercuts and hooks are especially effective, because they not only stress the muscles covering the abdomen, they squish the stuff inside around. In case you hadn't noticed, there ain't a whole lot of room for your guts to go wanderin' around in there. Things are tightly packed, so the heavier the blow, the more stress it puts on everything.

The structural flexibility of something can be used against it in confined areas. If it can't go anywhere, its flexibility can be turned against it by stressing it everywhere. Let me put it this way—if you hit a wall with your fist, the part you strike takes the most pressure. While there is energy bleed, the main stress point is still where your hand hits. If, however, you were to slam into a curb with a tire on your car, the pressure would stress out everything, but the tire would blow out at the weakest point. This is called a rupture. This same thing can be said about your guts when you get hit. Even if nothing blows in the confined area, everything gets stressed.

Most people, for some reason, forget they have an abdomen when they fight. Actually, they forget until someone slams an uppercut into their guts that makes them puff up like a bullfrog. Don't forget the abdomen in a fight. It's usually soft and unprotected. Rattlers and N.N.B.R.s are the ticket here. I personally prefer the knuckle-type blows, but a full-surface impact works pretty well, too.

The Kidneys and the Bladder

Moving around the back, we encounter an interesting little target used by streetfighters, but outlawed in boxing. The kidneys (oh, what a feeling). The kidneys are a secondary straining unit—little bags used by the body to strain out the stuff you need and then pass the rest out as toxins in the form of piss. In a sense, these little gumbies are a walking death sentence. Because of their job, if they're damaged, toxins leak into the system while much-needed nutrients pass out of the system. A N.N.B.R. to the kidneys can and will send somebody to the hospital. If a hospital is not reached, ruptured kidneys come down to an extremely painful way to end one's existence.

That sort of damage usually occurs with major impact, though. A lighter, faster punch to the old piss buckets is just out-and-out painful. I've been nailed there before, and let me tell you, children, it hurts like a mother. Anything that can get to somebody's kidneys should be used. Whether punch or kick, this is a real nut-numbing pain spot to get clobbered in.

Still part of the same system, but in the front, is the bladder. (Not quite the nuts yet, but close.) The bladder sits right up front and over the groin. This is another one of those potential death sentences that people don't know about. The bladder is basically a water balloon full of poison. Not a fun thought, I know, but true.

A whole lot of people don't make it away from car accidents because their bladders burst. This causes a thing called toxic shock syndrome. Not only are they wounded, but they're poisoned when the bladder bursts. Ugly. This is why I seriously advocate peeing before fights, especially if you have a full bladder. Not only does it hurt like a bitch when you're pegged there, but it can put you in the hospital right quick, if not the morgue. You may feel stupid standing there with pee running down your leg, but I guarantee that it feels better than the alternative.

Now that you know why you should protect it, let's look at what you can do to other people's pee pods. A biker I know by the name of Russ has a favorite trouble stopper that he uses. It's a Leopard Punch downward into the bladder. Just because you're standing doesn't mean you can't punch downward, got that? A knuckle punch does the same trick. Uppercuts, kicks, knees, elbows, and so on all work. Anything that puts pressure on the bladder is a good thing.

The Balls

Okay, here we are at long last! The balls! Trumpets, bells, and whistles! Tan ta de dah! Actually, I should say, "Well la de da . . . ." The balls are one of the most overrated targets in existence. It's not that they aren't good targets; they are. It's just something about the male psychological profile that makes covering the nuts the first normal reaction. Don't think this little bit of information hasn't crept into the streetfighter's world. It has.

A ball shot is one of the most expected, and therefore overrated, moves you can make. Every guy in the world expects the person that he's fighting to try and kick him in the balls. Men who attack women expect that as the first move. Barroom brawlers turn their gonads away when trouble starts. Most martial arts stances are designed to cover the old family jewels in some way. Face it, physical fighting is mostly a male-occupied industry. Because of this, the guys are worried about their dicks getting squished, plain and simple.

Unless the guy is really a twit (or he's young and

following biological patterns), he won't give you a ball shot as an opening move. The young part is simple. Young male conflicts usually follow preset patterns: puffing the chest, spreading the arms, jutting the chin, and standing toe-to-toe. The puffing and spreading is actually designed to take up more space and therefore to look bigger and more threatening. Basic aggressive biology here—the same reason dogs and cats puff up their hair. No lie. After this puffing match occurs, usually one or the other will deflate and back down. If neither backs down, it leads to a fight. It's after you've experienced a few kicks in the nuts because you were so busy putting your arms out behind you that you realize this stance is great for intimidation but a lousy way to start a fight.

The twit part can be one of two things. One, the guy really isn't a fighter and hasn't learned that it's not such a hot stance. Two, the guy is so confident that he has the upper hand that he's just blown it. This is the real twit. His overblown sense of superiority has just maneuvered him into a critical area if you're willing to act on it. Most of the time, this sort of guy doesn't think it's going to happen unless he's the one who starts it and finishes it. This can be a very dangerous misconception, especially around women and smaller men.

Most people don't want to fight, really. They'd rather walk away and let things slide. The twit who thinks it's not going to start without his calling the shots relies on this. He's going to push it until he's ready to attack, thinking that the other person is going to try and avoid violence until it's too late. Once you get out into the fighting world, though, you will discover that there are some people who have learned that they had better not let the other guy call the shots if they are going to survive. This is why you hear things like "look out for the little guy" and "watch out for quiet guys." These statements are made by people who know that in order to survive they have to get in and damage the other guy first.

In other words, if the guy thinks you're a fighter, he's not going to give you a ball shot. Don't even think of throwing one as your first move, because it's a waste of time. If, however, the guy thinks he's in total charge and it looks like he's the one who's going to initiate the violence, he may leave his nuts open because he's overconfident. If that's the case, move in when you have a chance. Once you sense his intent, if he gives you an opening, go for it. The odds, however, are against his giving you that easy ball shot up front. You may have to climb all over him first, then kick him as hard as you can, as many times as you can.

As I mentioned earlier, a whole lot of the pain that results from getting nailed in the nuts comes from your pelvis slamming into your spinal cord. But that is not all. Like the abdomen, they get squished. Ouch. They're supposed to be round, not pancaked. That's why even a glancing blow hurts. Unlike direct shots, glancing blows take a second or two to tell you that something is amiss in the kingdom. If you only give the guy a glancing blow, keep on coming—he'll realize it soon enough.

Another fun factor is that the scrotum, penis, and testicles are attached at one point. If you tug on the package, it strains the mooring lines (a polite way of saying you're going to be lying on the ground drooling and whimpering). This area is generally overlooked, and it can be very useful. The reasons are obvious, but most men have an aversion to grabbing another man's crotch. Get over it. If you slap a Dragon Punch on somebody's crotch and then squeeze and yank, he's going to squeal like a piggy. So not only do you have the serious kick to the balls, you have glancing blows that hurt, and anything from the Maimer lineup will really ruin the guy's day.

Now, how about *taking* a ball shot? (God, there are better things to do with your time.) The first thing you can do to keep the old family jewels intact is to pay attention to your footwork. Yes, most martial artists get nailed in the nuts because they get sloppy about their footwork, which is designed to cover your weblos to a certain extent. Second, spend lots of time practicing low blocks. Third, learn to watch the guy's shoulders. People move a certain way when they are about to kick. Number four has a lot to do with your mental state. You *can* live through a ball shot. You can't allow the pain to overwhelm you; you have to keep going. Keep this in mind, even when you want to just curl up and die. Number five is related to number four, but it has something to do with spirit. The Orientals call it the "one point." Most people who get kicked in the balls lose their one point. There's a belief that true fighting spirit comes not from the heart or the head, but down in the stomach. It explains why Ponce de Leon (the guy who explored the coast of Florida), whose name means "Stomach of the Lion," was not just suffering from a cruel joke by his parents. If you can find that part in your belly where this spirit comes from and hang onto it, you can take a ball shot like any other blow. This is what people are doing when they give demos about chi. Breaking boards is impressive, but having enough chi and control over your one point to take a ball shot and keep going is a little more practical.

An important thing to remember about some of the stuff that I say is that there is a whole lot of stuff going on outside as well as inside of you. It's important to remember that the Orientals were building cities and doing research into medicine and how the body works when many of our ancestors where hiding in the forest throwing rocks at hungry bears. Some of the stuff involved in fighting gets into downright mystical goo. I have never met an advanced fighter who doesn't accept some form of magic as part of his operating system. Things like chi, breathing, awareness, grounding, and balancing will all play into it. It's hard to explain some of these things without sounding like I'm talking about fairies and unicorns, but this stuff works. That's why I have to talk about strange-assed things like spirit, one point, and chi. There's just no other way to describe the stuff except in these weird terms. So, don't think that I've flipped out on you, or that I'm trying to convert you to some screwy religion. I'm not. I'm just sort of limited by the English language, which isn't designed to convey some of the necessary concepts.

You've probably caught on by now that to be a good fighter you have to be able to inflict damage while reducing the amount of damage you take. This comes from both knowledge and practice of the different type of strikes, blocks, shedding, balance, and mobility. Another thing you may have caught on to is that mental attitude will play a large part in how many fights you get into and what you do while you're there. This can include anything from stopping a situation before it develops (which is actually the best way) to having the ability to take a punch that would drop a normal person and keep on fighting. The latter is actually done one of two ways: you're so pissed that the adrenaline overrides the pain circuits, or you have so much mental discipline that you can actually shut off the circuits for a while. Either way, you pay for it later.

When I talk about this spirit that affects how you fight, it may sound like I'm going off to Lu-Lu land, but I'm not. This is a very real and powerful thing that you will encounter when fighting. The best warriors I know or have ever known all have something about them that can only be described as an inner peace. They're settled with the fact that they may die doing this. It's all right if they do, but they're going to give it their best shot to make sure it doesn't happen. That's why crossing these guys is such a bad idea; they're not afraid to die. Because of this, for some cockamamie reason, they're the ones who walk out unscathed most often. These are the people who walk their talk.

This spirit doesn't come out of a book, it comes from experience and miles traveled. In my books I try to give you some idea of where you can go with this stuff aside from just kicking ass. There's a whole mess of stuff lying beyond these lands. So know that you're headin' down a road with this stuff, even though you probably didn't intend to when you picked the book up.

CHAPTER SIX

The Limbs

It don't matter how big a guy is—if he can't walk, he can't get to you.

—An old streetfighter

There is a movie that I recommend to anyone who has any intention of surviving in this violent world of ours. It's *Roadhouse*, with Patrick Swayze and Sam Elliott. Not only does it offer some of the best advice on friendship and fighting, it contains some of the most realistic fighting scenes I've ever seen in a movie. One of the things that made me sit up and cheer (it annoyed the shit out of my lady, Tracy, because we were on the waterbed and she was drinking a soda, which was soon all over everything) was that it was one of the first movies I've ever seen that dealt with knee shots in a realistic manner (the first was *Billy Jack*).

Most movies spend very little time dealing with the limbs and what can be done with and to them. This is reflected in the public's idea of fighting. Joe Blow has no idea how vulnerable his limbs are in a fight. This is bad news for him and good news for you—if you know how to exploit this little oversight.

First, there are fighting styles that rely on using your limbs against you—judo, aikido, and jujutsu to start with. These styles are really effective on one main point: you have a choice of throwing yourself onto your head or getting a broken arm. Kali and some of the Chinese styles will cause you to wrap your arms around yourself in some weird-assed ways (trapping and binding, which I went into in *Cheap Shots*). What I'm going to deal with here are locks, binds, and twists that lead to popped bones or flattened heads. I'll also throw in some streetfighting to show you how to use blows against limbs.

The Arms

Let's start with impacts against the arms. As you know by now, the area where the arm meets the chest is a good target. Hit there and you are compressing joints, tendons, nerves, and arteries. There isn't much muscle there, but there's a lot of tender stuff. It won't stop the guy, but it will hurt him and slow him down. This is good. But don't forget that if you get nailed there, it will do the same to you. This is not good. So twist and roll to keep from getting hit there.

While it is technically possible to dislocate somebody's shoulder by striking there, you're more likely to have success with a Hanging Punch. The reason is that the shoulder is held in place by muscles—four major ones, to be precise. They cap the top of the humerus (upper arm bone) into your shoulder socket. The only place there isn't any real muscle holding the arm in place is on the underside, because the bone is there. Even so, the deltoid (the arm muscle that is usually counted as part of the shoulder) hangs on pretty damn tight, so you'd have to thump it a good one. As you can tell, it's not something you can just rush right out and do.

The next likely target on somebody's arm is the biceps muscle. For some cockamamie reason, the biceps seems to be thought of as the main indicator of strength in our culture. The biceps muscle is designed to pick things up. The weight-lifting exercise of "curling" is a perfect example of what the biceps does. So, other than getting food and beer to your mouth and picking up chairs so you can vacuum under them, the biceps do little else.

The triceps actually are the workhorses of the arm. They are of a muscle type called "extensors." Punching power comes from them. Getting hit by a guy with big triceps is a great way to see the universe (look at all the pretty stars). Biceps may look prettier, but they're less useful than triceps in fighting.

Where biceps do come in handy in fighting, though, is as targets. If you use reduced-area strikes against the guy's biceps, they're going to get bruised and slow him down. While the biceps are not exactly imperative to the striking process, since they're such close neighbors to the triceps, they can't help but get involved. If they're hurt, they'll hinder. Triceps are a little harder to reach, so you'll have to be content with Phoenix Punches to the front of the guy's arms.

The meaty part of the inner forearm has the same

potential for damage as the biceps, but as a target for a blow, it is about as effective as our justice system— you could spend a great deal of time trying and not actually get anything done except a lot of flailing about.

This is because when you hit the guy's forearm, it moves out of the way. The joints holding it there will give rather than stay and take punishment. In essence, you end up shoving the target away rather than actually hitting it. If you could catch his arm, you might be able to pop him a few times, but if you've got his arm trapped, go for more effective targets than his forearm, like nuts, abdomen, neck, or joints.

The way to get around that little problem and still deliver damage to the forearm is, believe it or not, with your blocks. The old streetfighter who taught me had the annoying habit (other than taking my best shots with an evil grin) of blocking my blows in such a way that he'd bruise the shit out of my arms. Quite natural-

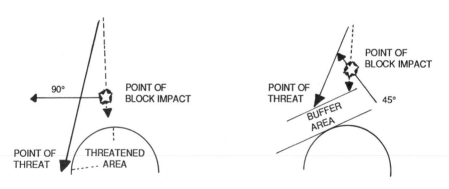

Left/right (ninety-degree) blocks against incoming force (at left) vs. deflecting forty-five degree blocks (at right). The ninety-degree block doesn't stop the forward motion of the point of threat until it's outside the target area. With the forty-five degree block, the point of threat never even gets close to the target.

ly, I insisted that he teach me how to perfect this little annoyance.

To sum it up, you block with the wrist and elbow. If nothing else, use the ulna (outer forearm bone) near the wrist. If you change the angle of your blocks from right to left in front of you to about forty-five degrees away and in front of you, you'll hit the more vulnerable fleshy parts. Check out the illustration and you'll see what I mean.

One thing that has always bothered me about karate blocks is that most of them consist of blocking left to right and up and down. Fencing and a few brawls taught me that technique is not the most effective way to stop a thrust. The closer you can get to a thrust's point of origin, the easier it is to deflect it out into the boonies. It also takes less energy to fuck up a blow closer to its source than it does to deflect it at the tip.

I explained whip and slap blocks in *Cheap Shots*. They can be really effective for maiming your opponent's forearm. Now I'm going to explain another useful block. There may be a proper name for it, but I've always called it the "chopping block." The chopping block is done from the elbow at the forty-five-degree angle I've been talking about. It doesn't involve the wrist except as a striking surface. About the best way to describe it would be to say that your forearm acts like a hammer striking a rubber band. Using your elbow as a pivot, you snap your forearm forward in an arc like a hammer (your fist being the hammer head). It's a sharp chop, actually. It doesn't matter if your hand or forearm hits your opponent's arm, it's the chopping action that does the damage. As you can see, your elbow joint can actually swing over a ninety-degree area with this action.

What this does is allow you to block an incoming blow while striking at the most tender part of your

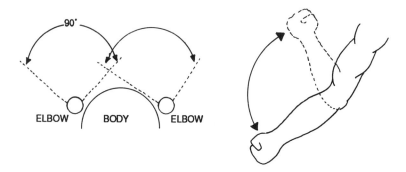

Ninety-degree strike area and pivoting action of elbow.

opponent's arms and legs (yes, it can work against kicks, too). If you block more at a forty-five-degree angle instead of left to right, you can do damage to the guy's arms and really slow him down. The reason this works better than a direct strike to the guy's arms is that his kinetic energy will hold him in place long enough for you to hurt him. What's more, if you use this block correctly, you can hit the guy on the inside of the elbow and fold his arm up like a piece of paper. So with this move, you not only hurt the guy's soft spots and possibly wrap him around himself, you can keep from getting hit.

In bare-handed fighting, the other guy's hands are sort of a waste of time as targets for striking. If the guy has a weapon, though, you had better learn how to pop his hands. Most people don't realize how vulnerable their grip on a weapon is. (Something else that amuses the hell out of me—if you knock a weapon out of someone's hand, he usually sits there and watches it fly away. No shit, it's true.) The reason that hitting the guy's hand when he's bare-handed is a waste of time is the same as when you're trying to hit his arm. There's nothing to hold it there, so it rolls with the force. The only exception to this is when you hit him in the hand as he's swinging. Then it's like a car crash and neither of you is going to walk away unhurt.

If, however, the guy has something in his hand and you peg his hand, the part you hit is going to be trapped between your incoming blow and the object in his hand. This is going to hurt his hand and possibly cause him to drop the weapon. Tonfas (the new billy clubs the cops are carrying) and nunchucks are really susceptible to this sort of attack. This is because with tonfas the guy has to loosen his grip to spin them, and with chucks, the energy of the flail can rip them out of the guy's grip when you stun his hand. If the guy has a knife in his hand, I suggest you throw something big and heavy, then run like hell. (Knives are the second most commonly used murder weapons in the United States. Handguns account for 50 percent; knives make up 20 percent.)

Legs

That's about it for blows against the arms; let's move down the legs. There are lots of muscles and bones down here, so the legs can take some serious damage before being affected. The femur (thigh bone) can withstand about two thousand pounds of pressure, making it the hardest bone to break in the human body. Okay, so that's out. You might be able to bruise the thigh muscles, which eventually would manifest in slowing and cramping. That can take some serious time, though. Come to think of it, 10-22 the entire thigh as an effective target. Let's move further south.

The knees! Oh, yes! Let's look at these wonderful little targets. First off, let's look at how the knees work. Basically, a knee is a one-way ball-and-socket joint that is limited from forward motion by the kneecaps and in backward motion by thigh and calf flesh.

Remember, this is how they work; anything else is painful.

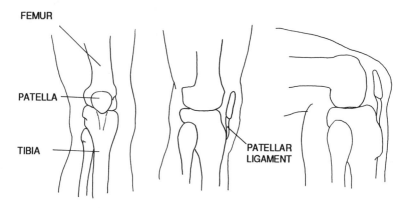

Front, side, and bent views of the knee and leg.

The main reason that I liked the moves in *Roadhouse* was that they came at the knees in a realistic way— from the side. This is the knee's weakest point and therefore the easiest way to bust it. The quickest way to pop somebody's knee is with a knife-edge kick. This is something else *Roadhouse* did right. You can blow somebody's knee with a roundhouse axe kick, but you have to be damned accurate. A courtesy roundhouse is a waste of time to try to use on somebody's knees. Stick kicks or any of the other N.N.B.R. kicks to the knee are another story. However, most people have to study for years before they get to that point in their kicking ability. To do somebody's knees from the side, it's more practical to stick with variations of knife-edge kicks.

Even if you don't break the guy's knee, he's going to have to bend to keep from getting it smashed. If his stance wasn't exactly good to begin with, the odds are that he's going to be hurting bad even without the busted knee. If, however, the guy's stance was good and he knew how to roll with it, a knee shot is not going to damage him that much. You can tell when you hurt somebody badly with a knee shot. There may be a loud snap, the guy might scream, his face could contort in agony, or all of these things could occur and he could fall down, too. This would be a prime opportunity for you to get the hell out of there (what I suggest) or move in and finish the job.

The important thing to remember is that if you didn't get those signals, but got the message the guy was rolling with your blow, don't rush in! There is a way to roll with a knee shot that trained fighters learn, which consists of rolling your knee in so it takes the impact on the back. This is something you should have your sensei teach you, because it is incredibly important. If you rush in on someone who knows this trick, he's in a perfect position to jam your nuts so hard that they'll blow up to your cheeks and make you look like a chipmunk.

Fortunately, this roll is not something most people know how to do. In fact, most people don't even think about guarding their knees. It comes back to that supply-line theme I was talking about earlier. If the guy can't breathe, see, or walk, he's not much of a threat, is he? You, on the other hand, had damn well better go out and learn this stunt, or the first savvy fighter you run across is going to hurt you bad.

That was the side of the knee. What about the front? It's harder to do anything with the front, because, for one, the guy has to lock his knee—or have it close enough to straight that it doesn't matter—for it to be broken effectively. The most effective way to take out the knee from the front is with a side kick using the knife edge of the foot. This way, you can get your entire weight behind the kick. Better and better.

Let's talk about blowing the guy's kneecap with a

front snap kick. The patella (kneecap) is held in place by cartilage and is designed to stop the leg from swinging too far forward. It's sort of flexible, so as to absorb shock when you step forward. That's why kicking it loose is such a bitch—it flexes if you don't hit it right. It can be done, but you have to be damn good or stone-cold lucky. Since I don't advise relying on luck in a fight, it falls back to being good. To do this stunt you have to be accurate, fast, and powerful. (Most people end up with a "choose two" situation out of that combo.) The kick only has to go in deep enough to shatter the kneecap; otherwise, the energy is absorbed by the femur and shin bone, and this defeats your purpose. On the other hand, if you can pop two-by-fours with a front snap kick, you might be qualified to do this, but as with any other display of super skill, the guy is not going to stand still while you do it. Besides, if you're that fast with a front snap kick, kick him in the nuts instead.

On to the shins. The tibia (shinbone) is another one of those stout, hard-to-break bones, but, like the temple, it hurts like hell if struck. All that pain without actually doing too much damage—fun, fun, fun. Taking the edge of your shoe and raking it down the guy's shin hurts like a bitch. The harder the shoe the greater the pain.

The feet are good targets for a couple of reasons. For one, if you stomp on the arch of somebody's foot hard enough, you're going to break it. Not step, *stomp.* That means you pick up your leg like you're going to try and pick your nose with your knee and then smash with the ball of your foot. It works because of the way the foot is constructed. Five foot bones, the metatarsals, are only slightly bent, and they hook up with another group of bones that make up the heel and the arch of your foot. If you break the seal between this latter group of bones and the metatarsals, you've just given the guy flat feet. It will hurt him. On the other hand, if he moves his foot or your aim is off, it will hurt you instead (so be careful when using this trick). By the way, this works better on concrete and asphalt. Grass and dirt act as shock absorbers to lessen the impact of your stomp.

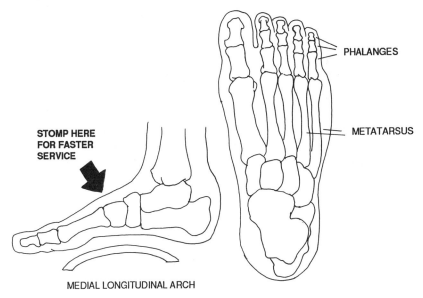

Foot bones.

Let's look at just stepping on the guy's foot. Try it some time with an understanding sparring partner. As you attack, step on his leading foot. If he is like most people, he will try and step away from your attack. There is usually a moment of confusion and unbalance when he discovers that you're standing on his foot and he can't exactly move as he had intended. If, however, you are up against somebody who is trained, in balance, and grounded, or who has encountered this move before, he will drag your ass with him, and *you* will be the one off balance. So be careful about applying this move.

I recently got a letter from a guy in Houston, Texas, who had a whole slew of questions. I answered them all, but one in particular stood out in my mind, namely because it was a damned good question. He asked if sweeps are any good. Well, I'm going to tell you the same thing I told him.

Sweeps are like any other tool. You must use them right for them to be effective. I told him to look at the movie *First Blood* for an example of an effective sweep. When what's-his-nuts was escaping from jail, he came across a guard in the entry of the police station. He swept the guy, busted his nose, and made good his escape. When he did this, the guard was still walking, or he was in the process of shifting into a stance to draw his gun; either way, it worked. One, the sweep hit the guy when he was off balance and when all of his weight was on one foot. That's the leg that got swept. Two, the sweep came from the outside of the load-bearing foot (in this case, the left side of the left foot). The guy would have had to cross over with his right leg to regain his footing (difficult, to say the least, and highly unlikely).

I've seen people try and do inside sweeps—the guy just shifts his weight to the other foot. It doesn't do shit and leaves you with your dick flapping in the wind. Another thing I've seen people do is to try and take out both feet at once. Highly unlikely, unless you're damn good. To do a sweep right, you have to pay a whole lot of attention to weight, mass, and centripetal and centrifugal forces. On top of everything else, you have to have your foot just right, or it drags into the dirt and mud and slows you down. Sweeps on the dojo floor are one thing; sweeps on asphalt are an entirely different subject. Tennis shoes are designed not to slip on asphalt, so it gets a little tricky.

The other thing I don't like about sweeps is that if the guy has seen one before, he knows what's coming. A sweep has only worked on me once. The guy swept me, and I got tangled up in his legs because he didn't finish getting out of there in time. I fell on him and pinned him down. Then, I crawled up his leg and beat the shit out of him. (By the way, it was done on a dirt and grass combo. He'd never done it outside of the dojo. I figure the ground is what really fouled him up.) Ever since then, when somebody starts to drop, I start to fly south for the winter. By the time the sweep gets to where I was, I'm airborne. So in general, I really don't advise sweeps.

Toes are fun. You can suck on your lover's toes and drive her wild (whether it's in ecstasy or because of ticklish feet depends on them), or you can block a kick and bust the guy's toes. Lots of people kick with their toes instead of with the balls of their feet. Not good, excluding cowboy boots and roach killers. (I think they're the same thing. Cowboys claim that the pointy-toed boot was invented by a bank robber who got caught because his square-toed boot missed the stirrup when he was trying to make his getaway. He invented them in prison, so he had a lot of experience killing cockroaches.) Oh yeah, and engineer boots. Those steel-toed monsters, if they land, can knock you into the next state. However, to get an effective kick off the starting line with those beasts, you need the help of N.A.S.A.

You don't want to kick with your toes because they break easily. My mother got pissed at me once and made a sudden move. I shifted into a stance, not even thinking about it. This enraged her more, and she said (and I quote), "Don't drop into a karate stance with me," at which point she kicked. This is also the point at which she broke her toe on my shin. We took her to the hospital only to discover that about all you can do with broken toes is tape them to a popsicle stick and let them be. She has busted her toe two more times since. Like noses, toes, once broken, are more susceptible to breaking again. (Both Mom and I have mellowed over the years, but I still find it funny.)

Anyway, if you find someone who is kicking with his toes, you might be tempted to let it land just to watch him hop around for a while. On the other hand, if you just block with the ball of your foot, the floor show's almost guaranteed.

That's enough on impact against the limbs. What about leverage, pressure, and out-and-out coercion? The hand is a wonderful thing. Because we have thumbs, we can do things like pick up beer cans, pinch girls' bottoms, hitchhike, and change the TV station. All in all, our thumbs are our greatest asset. (I've met people who were running neck-and-neck with apes, so I'm not counting the brain.) The thing about it is, the thumb can also be used against us. The way the thumb is attached to the hand makes it a great lever that you can use to do all sorts of neat things to a person's posture. If you grab somebody's thumb and twist it outward, the guy is going to throw himself on his head trying to keep you from breaking his thumb. The tendency to react this way is what judo, aikido, and jujutsu are based on. If you've ever had a run-in with the police and suddenly found yourself with your face mushed against the hood of a car and your arm sticking straight up behind you, you've encountered this particular gig.

Let's start with a look at the construction of the hand and wrist.

First, you have the finger bones. These are called

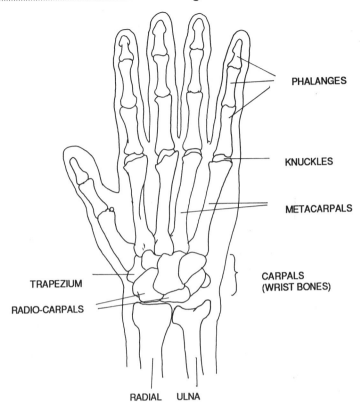

PHALANGES

KNUCKLES

METACARPALS

CARPALS
(WRIST BONES)

TRAPEZIUM

RADIO-CARPALS

RADIAL   ULNA

Hand and wrist bones.

the phalanges ("Ph" makes the "F" sound, so it sounds like "flanges" with an extra "A" in there somewhere). There are fourteen in each hand. They end where the knuckles are . . . and then the hand bones take over. These are called the metacarpals; we've got five per hand, and they are numbered one through five. Number one is the bone the thumb is attached to and number five is the pinky's bone. (Believe it or not, the thumb only has two bones. The other thing that hangs out with the thumb and moves around a lot is a metacarpal, or hand bone. I always called it my thumb, but it was pointed out to me that I was wrong. So fine, I can still break it off, no matter what I call it.) Moving down slightly, you encounter the wrist bones. These are called the carpals. There are eight of them, and in tandem, they allow you to do all sorts of neat moves with a tennis racquet (or whatever else you have in your hand). Each and every one has a name and a purpose. The only three we're going to look at here are two radio-carpals and the trapezium. The two radio-carpals meet your forearm bones, the ulna and radius. Oddly enough, the ulna radio-carpal connects to your ulna bone, and the radius radio-carpal to your radius. The trapezium is the one that connects to your first metacarpal. (Remember, the bone that used to be your thumb?) The back of the hand is called the dorsal side (ya know, like the fish fin?), and the palm is called the anterior side.

Now that I have everything defined, I'm going to shift over to Japanese. In aikido there is a move called ko da ghaish (pronounced "ko da guy shhh," and spelled I don't know how). From here on, I'm going to call it koda, and to hell with the guy-shit part. Basically, what koda is about is grabbing the hand in such a way that, by exerting pressure in a circular motion, you take the wrist to a place where it's not designed to go. From here on, the owner has the choice of having a busted wrist or throwing himself onto his head.

To do this little stunt, you need your fingers and your thumb. You can do it on yourself to a certain degree, but it works better on others. Important safety tip: be careful and gentle with your sparring partners. They are not the enemy. One of the most important things to remember about sparring partners is that they can and will hit back. I have seen—and heard many more accounts of—instances where people were unnecessarily rough on their sparring partners and got the living shit beat out of them for their indiscretion. If you hurt somebody because you're being careless or aggressive, it's nobody's fault but your own when you get a chair busted across your teeth. This is a serious breach of etiquette.

One of the things that people in the fighting world learn real quick is why etiquette came about in the first place. In an armed and dangerous society, being pushy and rude can get you killed. It's generally the people who don't have to put their asses behind their words and deeds that get really rude. Much of today's etiquette is no longer based on the "to keep your ass intact" premise; it has become a hollow shell full of pointless rules and regulations. But that's not how it started out. Originally, two armed guys had to figure out a way to behave so they wouldn't carve each other up over some small thing.

Real etiquette can be defined as the oil that society runs on. It gives you polite ways to deal with touchy subjects (like your sister screwing some guy—technically, it's none of your business, even if you feel differently). This is why etiquette is a handy thing. You know what's going on, you just don't have to notice it officially. This keeps everyone happy and alive. You don't have to push it, and you don't have to notice when somebody else is almost pushing it. Most dead bodies I've seen were the result of somebody pushing it too far one way or the other. (Remember, it becomes a different ball game when they shoot back.)

Now that I've done my Mr. Manners routine, let's get back to kicking ass. To do koda, you first put your palm on the dorsal side of your opponent's hand. Next, you crank your thumb in between the guy's fourth and fifth metacarpals (ring and pinky hand bones). The closer to the knuckles the better, but don't go too far or you'll slip off his knuckle and lose your grip entirely.

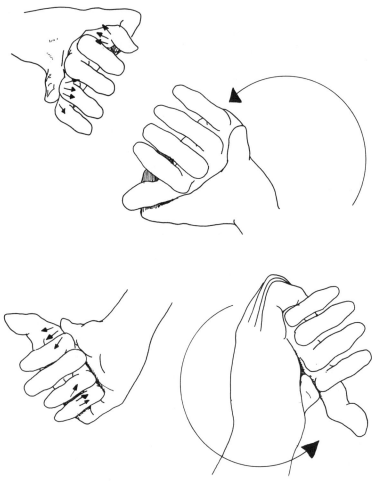

Two types of ko da ghaish: grabbing opponent's forearm with one hand and bending his wrist in with the other (top series); and bending the wrist inward while exerting pressure on the dorsal metacarpal (bottom).

Then, curl your fingertips around either his first or second metacarpal. Your fingers are the hook and your thumb is the lever. Got that? Now, twist his hand away from his body. For instance, if you've got his left hand, you twist in a clockwise motion (toward you), turning his wrist up and out to his left.

You can also put your thumb between his second and third metacarpals (index and middle hand bones). Wrap your fingers around his fifth metacarpal. From here, the motion is downward and out in a circle. If it's his left hand in your right hand, you twist counterclockwise, with your thumb doing the pushing out. (The problem with this form is that it's easier to get out of than the first one. If he snaps his hand down and to his left, he slides out of your hand like a greased catfish.)

I would like to point out something that both Peyton Quinn and I agree on. Lots of judo-type moves work a whole lot better if you pop the guy a few times before you try and lock his joints up. Rattle his teeth a few times before you try and lead him somewhere. He'll follow a lot easier that way.

These moves work because they put pressure on the radius and ulna radio-carpal bones in some unpleasant ways—rotation and leverage. If you bend the wrist in, it only goes so far, right? If, while bending the wrist, you apply pressure on the dorsal metacarpal, you've effectively pinned the wrist. This works best if you use two hands on the guy. One move is where you grab his forearm with one hand and bend his wrist in with the other. This is limited because the guy can still swing, which he may try to do until you place some more pressure on his hand; then he'll probably repent.

The other move is the infamous police armlock. You bend the wrist inward while exerting pressure on the dorsal metacarpal. While all of this is happening, muckle onto the back of his elbow with your outer hand. By pushing it down, you lock the elbow joint open. This gives you the option of breaking either the elbow or the wrist. Actually, if you're really annoyed, elbow or the wrist. Actually, if you're really annoyed, you can take out both.

Now there are two ways to do this—the "right" way and the "this is the best that I can manage at the moment" way. The right way is to catch his hand with a koda-type move. Then, in about eight different moves, you rotate his wrist inward and back so his fingers are pointing the same way his elbow is. From the elbow, you apply pressure and lead him around, possibly onto the hood of a car. This is the classic police armlock. The guy will go wherever you want him to.

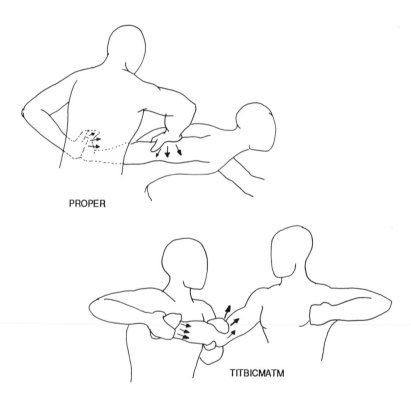

PROPER

TITBICMATM

Proper police wrist lock and "This is the best I can manage at the moment" (TITBICMATM).

The approach is a little different. The wrist is still turned in, but it's not rotated to the outside. You've still got him by the elbow though. His own skeleton has got him pinned in place. If he tries to strike, you can pop his wrist easier than you can his elbow.

Moving back to the thumb and its pet metacarpal for a moment, we realize that it is a great joystick. If you grab a guy's thumb and rotate it out, you can either pop his radio-carpals or his trapezium (the carpal the thumb metacarpal is attached to). In other words, all that fancy shit aside, you could break his wrist or his thumb. It's better to rotate the thumb outward than to try folding it back against the forearm. While both ways work, rotating is easier.

Moving right along, we get to the phalanges. (Fingers, remember? The singular form of phalanges is phalanx. Sort of like the singular of mice is moose . . . er . . . mouse.) These are handy little things in an interesting way. Take your finger and fold the last two bones over. The third bone, or the fingertip, should be on your palm. With the finger of your choice from your other hand, press the bent finger into its own palm. It doesn't really do much, does it? Now, take the palm of your other hand and place it against the second knuckle of that same bent finger. Reach over with your thumb and pin down the tip. For the next step, push the finger down into your palm and drag the tip back into the third knuckle so the helpless little guy is pushed down into its own palm and dragged screaming toward the palm of your other hand. Hurts, doesn't it? With a slight variation, you can do the same thing with the thumb. You just fold it up and try and stuff it down where the wrist is. That one is no picnic, either.

The last way to foul up somebody's hand is really simple. Grab a finger and bend it backwards. If you can grab at the second knuckle and immobilize it, you can break the first phalanx from the metacarpal at the joint. Breaking anything is easier at the joint.

There's something I should have put in earlier. In *Cheap Shots,* I said you should never lock your elbow when you punch. Since then I have heard all sorts of reports on the physics of punching and why you can increase impact power by locking your elbows, blah, blah, blah. Actually, it's true. You can. But before you go running off and start locking your elbow, read this.

If I throw a punch with my elbow bent and the guy catches my arm, I could be in some deep shit, mostly from a kick in the balls. In order to break my arm, however, he's going to have to hit directly onto the back of my elbow and bend it back at least ninety degrees from the way it's supposed to go. A number of small muscles around the elbow keep everything there in line, and the biceps keeps my arm from extending all the way when I

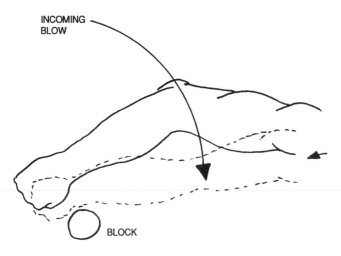

INCOMING
BLOW

BLOCK

Overhead view of incoming blow with curved elbow. Dotted line indicates how far the arm must be pushed before any chance of breaking is present.

don't want it to. My humerus bone seats into my shoulder socket, where a number of muscles keep it from wandering around the countryside. Now that we know all of the players, let's look at a team picture.

If the guy strikes, he has to straighten out a number of contracted smaller muscles, as well as my biceps. This calls for an amount of energy that most people can't muster very effectively. Let us take a gander up at the humerus bone. Big bone, ain't it? It can take a lot of strain. It's seated into a socket that leads to the rib cage and shoulders. This means it can take the blow, absorb it, and pass it on to the structure. It's gonna take a whole hell of a lot of energy to overcome the shoulder muscles and the structural brace. (Face it, the odds are against it ever happening.)

Let's look at a locked elbow. Everything is extended.

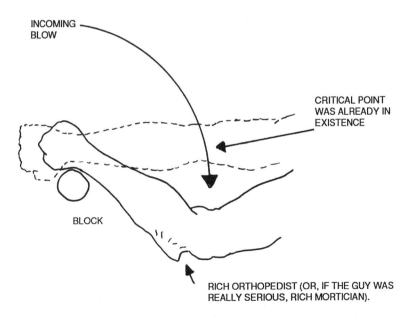

Locked elbow and the force needed to break it.

There is no muscle contraction to overcome. With it locked and held straight out from the body, the shoulder can't act as a force-absorbing structure. The only things keeping it in place are the socket and some fascia tissue. Come in at a ninety-degree angle and you can blow that sucker.

Do you understand now why I really object to the locked-elbow theory? I really do feel it is a good way to get hurt, and the object of this book is to keep you from getting hurt in a fight.

The pipe is the symbol of the Universe. When you use the pipe, you are using the Authority of the Universe, that part of the Universe that is within you. Your Ego has no place within that Authority. It is you and the Universe, not only existing with each other, but being one.
                              —Conversation with an Indian medicine man

One of the greatest joys I get out of writing these books is that every now and then somebody sits down and writes me a letter telling me how much they appreciate what I'm writing. They're usually guys who are going through a really tough time and who feel very alone out there. What they're feeling and seeing doesn't gel with what they're being told by society, teachers, parents, friends, or whomever else they listen to. Then along comes little ol' me saying, "Yeah, not only that but did you see this?" The greatest compliment I've ever gotten about my writing is that "it saves people's asses." I talk about stuff that nobody else does, and I think it's damned important to drag these things out into the open.

Face it, it's a big, wild, scary world out there. If you don't know what's what and who's where, you can get nailed pretty hard. All you have to do is look around and see the human wrecks that have washed up on the shores of humanity to realize you must do something to keep from ending up seriously damaged. Washing behind your ears and saying your prayers every night just doesn't cut it anymore.

They tell you "keep your nose clean" and "don't ask those kinds of questions." It works, until the day you accidentally find yourself in territory where you've never been before. Suddenly, it's a whole lot more complicated than just keeping your nose clean and going to work every day.

Life's a journey, and even if you don't think you're going anywhere, you're prone to drift. A lot of times, you end up drifting into some hard-core territories; if you're not ready for them, they'll eat you alive. Violence is one such territory. Once you've gone through it, you know it. And once you really know it, it's not so terrifying anymore. Best of all, you can learn to avoid it altogether. Part of what constitutes knowing it is seeing it coming down the line. If you see it coming, you can avoid it or let it know that all it'll get from you are hard knocks, so it had better go hunting trouble elsewhere. If you don't intentionally go through the territory, though, you'll never know when you're drifting toward it. And if you don't know about it, it'll reach up and grab you from a blind side. Violence is something whose embrace you may not survive.

What's the line? Oh, yeah, "You fucked with death, now it's your wife."

Personally, I have always maintained that once you know that something is dangerous, that makes it less dangerous. It doesn't mean it's not dangerous, it just means that you're less likely to get caught with your pants down.

I have a friend who got shot a few years ago. He was taking out the garbage in New York City and dumped it into a city trash can. Some guy yelled at him, and in true New York fashion he told the guy to fuck off. He then walked across the street to a liquor store. When he turned around, the guy was waiting with a gun. Bang.

The hardest thing about that is my friend is not a fighter. In fact, he's a writer. It was a total shock to him. Violence was not something that happened to him. He spent some years putting it back together.

On the other hand, I have another friend who got shot who was a fighter. He was walking home and was confronted by a couple of guys who were pledges to a gang. The initiation was to go out and shoot someone. They picked the wrong guy. As he heard the gun cock he threw himself sideways and drew his knife. The bullet went through his left arm as he was stabbing the guy with his right. I saw him a few days later and asked what was happening, and he laughingly told me he had been shot. I didn't believe him until he showed me the bullet hole. We still joke about it to this day.

Those are two extremes. I've been hurt in fights and cut with blades, but now I've mellowed out. I've got my old lady, and I'm settling in. Shit still comes down the pikeway at me now and then, but it is seldom violence. People look at me, see the Warrior's Mark, and move along. There are easier people to tangle with. Violence will never be a surprise to me again. I can see it coming down the highway long before it ever gets to me. What's more, it sees me watching it and knows I've got its number. It's no guarantee, but nine out of ten times, it moves on.

I'm not afraid of violence, I'm not surprised by it anymore, but I just don't want to do it anymore. This is what I mean by knowing the territory. It's not a game, and once you know it and how it works, you can get on with the other things in your life. (Like women—hell, you're going to spend most of your life trying to figure them out anyway.)

I know how terrifying violence is. For years the very thought of it would send me off into spasms of machismo trying to prove that I wasn't about to wet myself. I knew that I had gone a little too far, though, when the last time somebody shot at me, I got mad instead of scared. Not a good place to be.

A big reason why I write these books is so you can learn these things without having them sprung on you from a blind spot. If you know these things up front, you can get out of the territory a whole lot quicker and into someplace that's a whole lot more fun and interesting. Violence, like chaos, has a habit of consuming its disciples. Face it, that shit just ain't worth it.

It's your life, make it as good as you can. Not only is it more fun, but you can get a whole lot more out of it than somebody who's trapped in the bullshit.

Fly low and stay cool.

—Animal